Beginning Broadcast Newswriting:

A Self-Instructional
Learning
Experience

THIRD EDITION

Beginning Broadcast Newswriting:
A Self-Instructional Learning Experience

THIRD EDITION

K. TIM WULFEMEYER

IOWA STATE UNIVERSITY / AMES

K. TIM WULFEMEYER is professor, Department of Journalism, San Diego State University, where he teaches broadcast newswriting, reporting, and production. He has worked for radio and television stations in California, Iowa, New Mexico, Texas, and Hawaii. Dr. Wulfemeyer has degrees from San Diego State University, Iowa State University, and the University of California at Los Angeles and is the author of *Broadcast Newswriting: A Workbook* and *The News Blues: Problems in Journalism.*

LORI LYNN McFADDEN WULFEMEYER assisted in the writing and editing of this book. She has a bachelor's degree from Iowa State University and a law degree from the University of Hawaii. She has taught at San Diego State University and the University of Hawaii and has worked for radio and television stations in Iowa, California, and Hawaii.

First edition, 1976
   Second printing, 1978
   Third printing, 1979
   Fourth printing, 1981
Second edition, 1984
   Second printing, 1990
   Third printing, 1991
Third edition, 1993

Library of Congress Cataloging-in-Publication Data

Wulfemeyer, K. Tim
   Beginning broadcast newswriting: a self-instructional learning experience / K. Tim Wulfemeyer.—3rd ed.
      p.   cm.
   Includes bibliographical references.
   ISBN 0-8138-0211-3
   1. Broadcast journalism—Authorship. I. Title.
PN4748.B75W8   1993
808'.06607—dc20

Back cover quote: Dr. Folu Ogundimu, Journalism Department, Michigan State University

Contents

Preface, vii

Introduction, viii

Part 1. Writing the Story, 3

Rewriting, 3
  Be Original, 3
Short, Lean Sentences, 3
  Short but Sweet, 3
  Trim the Fat, 4
Brevity, 4
  Make It Brief, 4
  Tight but Not Constricting, 5
Helping the Listeners, 5
  One to a Customer, 5
  Nickel and Dime the Listeners, 6
Tell the Story, 6
  Talking It Out, 6
Read the Story, 6
  Eyeing It Up, 6
Summary, 7
  One More Time, 7

Part 2: Using Broadcast Style, 8

Leads, 8
  Did You Hear the One About . . . ? 8
  Lead On, 9

No Questions, 11
  Choose a Lead #1, 12
  Choose a Lead #2, 14
  Choose a Lead #3, 15
  Choose a Lead #4, 17
Names and Titles, 21
  What's in a Name? 21
  Who Was That? 21
  Endless Titles, 22
  First Names First, 23
  Eliminate the Middleman, 23
  The Name Game, 24
  Answers to the Name Game, 25
Identification, 26
  Identification Please, 26
Addresses, 26
  Home Sweet Home, 26
Ages, 26
  Age Gracefully, 26
Attribution, 27
  Who Says So? 27
  Attribution Test #1, 29
  Answers to Attribution Test #1, 30
  Say It with *Says,* 30
Repetition, 30
  Repeat, Repeat, Repeat, 30
Quotes, 31
  Quotable Quotes, 31
  Close but No Cigar, 32
  Quotations Test, 33
  Answers to Quotation Test, 34
Facts or Opinions? 35

To Attribute or Not To Attribute, 35
Attribution Test #2, 36
Answers to Attribution Test #2, 37
Aiding the Listeners, 38
Half-Listening Listeners, 38
Contractions, 38
Contractions Can't Hurt, 38
Pronouns, 39
Who's He? 39
You Is Us, 39
Verb Tense, 40
Now Is the Time, 40
Time Elements, 40
Timely Time, 40
Natural Time, 41
Verb Voice, 41
Action Please, 41
Rewriting, 43
Rewriting Test, 43
Answers to Rewriting Test, 44
Abbreviations, 46
What Does T-H-A-T Stand For? 46
Organized Organizations, 46
A R-O-S-E Is Not a ROSE, 47
Abbreviations Test #1, 48
Abbreviations Test #2, 50
Answers to Abbreviation Test #2, 52
Numbers, 53
By the Numbers, 53
Ban the Symbols, 53
Ordinary Ordinals, 54
Bits and Pieces, 54
Round Figures, 54
Telling Time, 55
Exceptions to Numbers Rules, 55
Numbers Test #1, 56
Numbers Test #2, 58
Answers to Numbers Test #2, 60
Approximation Test, 61
Answers to Approximation Test, 62
Punctuation, 63
Practical Punctuation, 63
Copyediting, 63

Correctable Errors, 63
Script Style, 64
Putting It on Paper, 64
Summary, 65
Play It Again, 65
The BIG Time, 66
Exercises, 67
Komodo Dragons Story, 67
Komodo Dragons Story Model, 68
Traffic Fatality Story, 69
Traffic Fatality Story Model, 70
Cancer Money Story, 71
Cancer Money Story Model, 72
Sports Arena Story, 73
Sports Arena Story Model, 74
Supervisor Controversy Story, 75
Supervisor Controversy Story Model, 76
USO Story, 77
USO Story Model, 78

Part 3: Adding Visuals, 79

Writing for Television, 79
Turn on the TV, 79
Split Screen, 81
Exercises, 82
Westlake High School Story, 82
Westlake High School Story Model, 83
SAT Scores Story, 84
SAT Scores Story Model, 85
Measles Shots Story, 87
Measles Shots Story Model, 88
Delayed Debate Story, 90
Delayed Debate Story Model, 91
Summary, 93
Once Again, Dear Friends, 93
Congratulations, 94
Additional Reading, 94

Appendix, 95
United Press International Pronunciation Guide, 95

Preface

This book will help you to become familiar with some of the basic styles, principles, and techniques of broadcast newswriting. To complete most of the exercises, all you'll need is a pencil or pen and some blank sheets of paper. A cassette tape recorder would be helpful in this learning experience, but it's not necessary.

Follow the instructions in the book carefully. You won't be reading through it page by page; you'll be skipping pages and perhaps even rereading pages. Pay close attention to all directions, but especially those at the bottom of some pages.

Take a look at the following list of skills you'll have learned when you've finished this book. Using correct broadcast news style, you'll be able to:

1. Write radio and television news "reader" stories.

2. Place attribution in its proper place in a sentence.

3. Place a person's title in its proper place in a sentence.

4. Place a person's age in its proper place in a sentence.

5. Place a person's address in its proper place in a sentence.

6. Write direct and indirect quotations.

7. Place time elements in their proper place in a sentence.

8. Write numbers.

9. Write individually voiced numbers and letters.

10. Write copy to match pictures and graphics.

11. Write copy to match video.

12. Edit copy.

Introduction

In broadcast newswriting, you're writing for the ear and the eye, not just for the eye as in newspaper writing. A newscaster has to be able to read your copy easily, so you have to make it easy on the eye. And it has to *sound* good to your listeners, so you have to make it easy on the ear, too.

Writing for both the ear and the eye is a tricky business. It takes skill and practice to explain complicated issues and events in understandable, simple words, but that's what the broadcast newswriter must do.

Most stories must be told in 15 to 30 seconds. Some very important or complicated stories run a little longer, but rarely does any one story run longer than two minutes on the average broadcast news program. It's not easy to write a clear, understandable story in simple, direct language that gives the important elements of an event or issue in less than two minutes, and it's especially difficult to accomplish the task in less than 30 seconds.

The most successful broadcast newswriters write the way people talk in their everyday conversations. Conversational writing is the key. It's the secret of good broadcast newswriting. Just remember, when you're writing a broadcast news story, THINK the way you talk and WRITE the way you talk.

Try to write the story the same way you'd tell it to a friend. Think of the entire audience as just one of your friends and write the story as you'd tell it to him or her personally. If you can do that, you're on the way to becoming a professional broadcast newswriter.

This book will give you some tricks of the trade, guidelines, hints, and suggestions that can help you become a successful broadcast newswriter.

Beginning Broadcast Newswriting:
A Self-Instructional Learning Experience

THIRD EDITION

PART 1

Writing the Story

- ## REWRITING

Be Original

As a broadcast newswriter, it's mandatory that you understand the material and information you're writing about before you start writing. A great deal of broadcast newswriting is actually rewriting—rewriting wire copy, news releases, scripts, and handwritten notes.

Whatever information source you use, the important thing is to understand it. If you don't understand it, how can you hope to write a story that your listeners will understand? Look for the basic elements of journalism—the who, what, where, when, why, and how. They'll help you begin to organize your story.

A good practice is to read over the source copy a couple of times, put it aside, and try to tell the story to another person or say it to yourself. After you've done that, then go ahead and start writing.

Try not to look back at the source copy. Tell the story in YOUR OWN words, not someone else's. Every other radio station, television station, and newspaper in your community will more than likely use stories covering the same material. You want your story to sound different from all the others. The only way to do that is by telling the story in YOUR words.

Don't simply retype or rearrange the words and sentences used in the source copy. Tell the story in your own words. You can make it more conversational and easier to understand. Your version doesn't always have to be *better* than the original, but it should always be *different* from the original.

- ## SHORT, LEAN SENTENCES

Short but Sweet

One way to improve source copy is to shorten the sentences. A good average length for broadcast news sentences is about 20 words. But avoid the choppy and stilted style of "See Spot run. Run, Spot, run."

3

Create a flow and rhythm to your copy—a natural, conversational flow and rhythm. Sentences should flow easily without abrupt changes in topic and without awkward pauses and phrasing.

Alternate long sentences with short ones. Alternate the simple declarative sentences with sentences starting with *and, but,* or *because*. People talk this way, so you should write this way. As long as it *sounds* okay and as long as it's conversational, use it. The subject-verb-object sentence is best for clarity and directness. Stay away from clauses and phrases that sound unnatural. Not many people start a sentence with a phrase. It just doesn't sound right.

Example (poor): Speaking before a group of Midcity University students, State Senator Sam Bergman today announced his candidacy for governor.

Does the above example *sound* natural to you? Probably not. You don't talk that way, so don't write that way.

Example (better): State Senator Sam Bergman today told a group of Midcity University students that he's going to run for governor.

Remember, write the way you talk.

Trim the Fat

Write lean sentences, NOT fat sentences. A lean sentence is one that's trimmed of all excess words, especially adverbs and adjectives and other qualifiers that can distort what happened or what was said. Let your verbs provide the action and the color in your writing.

Avoid such words as *beautiful, ugly, hurriedly, frantically, slowly, smug, excitedly, sad,* and *good*. This doesn't mean your writing has to be stripped down to the bone. Just avoid the "value judgment" adverbs and adjectives. Your judgments might not match those of your listeners.

Be accurate in your descriptions. If a woman wears a "red" dress, write she was wearing a "red" dress. Don't write she was wearing a "beautiful, flaming red, exquisitely designed dress."

What is beautiful, flaming, and exquisitely designed to you might be ugly, dull, and tasteless to someone else.

• BREVITY

Make It Brief

Time limitations are among the greatest handicaps to the broadcast newswriter. Not only are you often on deadline, but you also must keep your stories to less than 30 seconds. You simply don't have enough time to write all you'd like to write about every story. You have to get to the news, explain why it's news, and give as many important details as possible in the limited time available.

You have to cut out all the frills and get right to the heart of each story. Be as brief and concise as you can while still including all the necessary facts.

Tight but Not Constricting

In your efforts to trim the fat from your story and to be brief, be sure you don't omit necessary detail. Don't sacrifice meaning for brevity. Don't distort or leave out what's essential.

You have to be an editor. Decide what is important for your listeners to know and share it with them. Don't forget to explain WHY things are important and WHY things happen. Point out the significance. Explain the meaning. Tell your listeners how events, issues, and developments will affect them. Answer the question, "So what?"

Include the causes and results of events, issues, policies, and statements. WHY are phone bills going up? WHY are the garbage collectors on strike? WHY is the economy in trouble?

Be sure to give your listeners the reasons behind actions. Include all the important details. Your job is to explain complex events in a concise manner using understandable language. Do a thorough, professional job.

● HELPING THE LISTENERS

One to a Customer

When you're trying to report the complete story, don't cram your sentences with a jumble of separate facts. The old "summary lead" works reasonably well for newspaper and magazine stories, but it's rarely appropriate for broadcast news stories. Limit most of your sentences to one idea, fact, or image. It can become confusing when you start crowding different concepts, facts, and elements of a story into a single sentence.

Take each part of the story one step at a time—one sentence at a time. When you limit sentences to one main point each, you give your listeners a chance to hear and understand all the elements of the story.

When you pack your sentences with a number of points, your listeners are bound to miss some of them. Remember, listeners can't go back and relisten as readers can go back and reread something they miss or don't understand the first time.

Listeners have to get the information on the first shot, or they don't get it at all. Taking the elements of each story one at a time—a sentence at a time—gives your listeners the best chance of getting the information they should get.

Example (poor): Governor Bonner says he paid only 50-dollars in state income taxes last year, because he suffered heavy losses in the stock market and donated his gubernatorial papers to Midwest State University where officials set the value of those papers at more than 300-thousand-dollars.

Lots of separate facts have been crowded into that one sentence. So many, in fact, that it's hard to understand them all. A rewrite of Governor Bonner's tax problems could help simplify the issue.

Example (better): Governor Bonner says he paid only 50-dollars in state income taxes last year for two main reasons. First . . . he suffered heavy losses in the stock market. And second . . . he donated his gubernatorial papers to Midwest State University. The University estimates those papers are worth about 300-thousand-dollars.

Nickel and Dime the Listeners

Another way to help your listeners understand all the elements of your story is to use simple and direct words—the "nickel and dime" words. The big, impressive-sounding, multisyllabic, "10-dollar" words don't belong in broadcast newswriting.

"The simpler the better" should be your motto, because the simple words are the ones more people will understand. Take a look at the following list of words. See if you don't agree that the simple words are the better words for broadcast newswriting.

Use	Don't Use
anger	indignation
send	transmit
buy	purchase
show	exhibit
need	require
cuts	lacerations
dead	deceased
try	attempt
enough	sufficient
home	residence
give	contribute
question	interrogate
see	witness
use	utilize

• TELL THE STORY

Talking It Out

While writing your story, it's a good idea to say the sentences out loud before you write them on paper or put them into the computer. If you talk your story out—or at least say it to yourself—and it sounds simple and understandable to you, it's a good bet that your listeners will understand it, too.

After you've finished writing your story, read it out loud. Listen to how it *sounds*. Be sure it says what you want it to say. Be sure you sound as if you're *telling* a story, not *reading* a story.

• READ THE STORY

Eyeing It Up

Although much of the emphasis in broadcast newswriting is on writing copy that's easy on the ear, you should remember that somebody—you, a newscaster, or a sportscaster—has to *read* that copy. You have to make your copy easy on the eye as well as easy on the ear. You'll need to follow the rules we've already covered, plus all the ones to come in Part 2.

A little later we'll be going over some specifics on how to write words and numbers so they're easy for a newscaster to read. We'll also cover how to provide pronunciation guides and how to edit a script.

The important thing to remember is to write your stories so the newscaster can read them easily and the listeners can listen to them and understand them easily.

● SUMMARY

One More Time

Here's a quick summary of the general hints for broadcast newswriting that we've covered so far.

1. Be original. Tell the story in your own words. Don't parrot source copy.

2. Use short sentences, but create a flow to your writing—a natural, conversational flow.

3. Trim the excess fat of needless words, especially adjectives and adverbs.

4. Be as brief and concise as you can.

5. Write tightly, but don't sacrifice meaning. Be sure to include the WHY, the significance, and the meaning of the story.

6. Don't cram your sentences full of facts. Take the elements of each story one at a time—a sentence at a time.

7. Use the "nickel and dime" words, not the "10-dollar" words. Use words that are easy to say, easy to listen to, and easy to understand.

8. Talk your story out. Make sure it *sounds* right.

9. Make your stories easy on the eye as well as easy on the ear. Make it easy for a newscaster to read your copy, and make it easy for your audience to listen to and understand your copy.

10. Think and write the way you talk.

P A R T   2

Using Broadcast Style

- **LEADS**

  ### Did You Hear the One About . . . ?

  Now that we've talked about broadcast newswriting in general, it's time to get down to some specifics. Probably the most important part of a broadcast news story is the first sentence or the first couple of sentences. If you don't get the listeners' attention at the beginning, all your fact gathering and all your careful writing will have been for nothing.

  The first part of the story is called the *lead*. The lead should tell the listeners what the story is going to be about. It's kind of like a headline in a newspaper. It sets the tone of the story. It captures the flavor of the story. It characterizes the story.

  The lead is what you'd say right after you met a friend. "Hi Jack, guess what happened today." Or "Guess what I saw." Or "Have you heard?" The THING that happened, the THING you saw, or the THING you heard is the lead.

  Example: Jill, have you heard? Mayor Alvarez resigned today.

  Example: Jack, guess what? All our teachers have gone on strike, so we won't have school tomorrow.

  Example: Jill, did you hear? Three people died in a plane crash at the airport this afternoon.

  Just try to tell the most important part of the story right at the start. After you do that, the rest of the story should fall into place without too much trouble. Once you have the lead, fill in the details and explain the significance—what the story means and how it affects people.

Lead On

There are many different types of leads, but four of the most common are the emphasis lead, the umbrella or blanket lead, the verbless lead, and the chronological or narrative lead.

The *emphasis lead* is the one we've already talked about. You pick out the most important part of the story and emphasize it by using it at the beginning. It's generally the WHO, WHAT, and WHEN of the story.

Example: Mayor Alvarez resigned this morning.

Mayor Alvarez is the WHO. *Resigned* is the WHAT. *This morning* is the WHEN.

Sometimes the WHERE of the story is one of the most important elements.

Example: More fighting in the Middle East today.

Example: Bombs hit London again this evening.

Example: A hurricane crashed into Hawaii this morning.

The WHY of most stories, although important, is usually saved for later in the story, because it often takes time to explain it fully. But be sure to include the WHY whenever you can.

Example (poor): Midcity Power says it's cutting back home heating oil allotments by 25-percent. That means about 20 gallons a month less for the average family.

Without the WHY, this story is incomplete. Listeners will want to know why the oil was cut back, so tell them.

Example (better): Midcity Power says it's cutting back home heating oil allotments by 25-percent. That means about 20 gallons a month less for the average family. The cutback is being blamed on the OPEC boycott.

The second type of broadcast news lead is the *umbrella* or *blanket lead*. It's general instead of specific. It covers a number of things or a number of elements, but all of the separate parts are related in some way.

Example: The U-S Supreme Court ruled on three landmark cases this afternoon.

After you've let the listeners know that you're going to be telling them about three things and not just one, you can start filling in the details.

Example: The U-S Supreme Court ruled on three landmark cases this afternoon. It ruled that all the nation's obscenity laws are unconstitutional . . . that animals have legal rights . . . and that states can't require automobile license fees.

See how an umbrella or blanket lead can group a series of separate but related stories into one neat package? One caution, however: Be sure all the stories belong under the same umbrella or blanket. Don't force the groupings. Avoid strange bedfellows.

Take a look at a couple of good blanket leads.

Example: Plenty of debate . . . but little action at the Board of Education meeting this afternoon. (Follow with details of the debates and why there was no action.)

Example: Three Midcity people died in separate traffic accidents over the weekend. (Follow with the facts of each accident.)

The third type of broadcast news lead is the *verbless lead*. It gets its name from the fact that no verb is used.

Example: Two more traffic deaths last night.

Example: A busy day at City Hall.

Use verbless leads sparingly, though. Complete sentences (subject–verb–object) are usually better, because that's the way we talk.

The fourth type of broadcast news lead is the *chronological* or *narrative lead*. You start writing with the first thing that happened and follow with the rest of the details in the order they happened.

Example: Tonight started out like any other night for Terri Kegel. She's the owner of the Cut-Rate gas station on Broadway. But about nine o'clock . . . two men drove in . . . poked a gun in her ribs . . . and took all her oil. That's right . . . oil. No money . . . just oil.

You probably won't use a narrative lead very often, but it is good for funny and light-hearted feature stories. Generally, you don't have enough time to give a chronological blow-by-blow account, so start your story with information that would logically follow, "Guess what I just heard."

No Questions

An overworked, overused, and unnatural-sounding lead is the *question lead*. You've probably heard millions of them.

Example: Are you tired and run-down?

Example: Do you want to know how to get ahead in life?

Commercials use question leads all the time. You don't want your listeners to think your story is going to be a commercial, so stay away from question leads. Besides, people tune to broadcast newscasts for answers, not more questions. Your lead should answer the unasked but implied question, Have you heard?—not ask another question.

If you want a question-type lead, modify it for broadcast news.

Example (poor): Are you looking for ways to save money on food? Well, we have some hints for you.

Example (better): If you're looking for some ways to save money on food . . . we have some hints for you.

Turn to page 12 to compare some leads.

Choose a Lead #1

Now that we've gone over some of the ways to write broadcast news leads, let's take a closer look at some examples. If you have a tape recorder handy, record the two leads on this page and play them back. If you can't record them, then look them over and decide which one would be better for broadcast news.

1. General Motors Corporation has announced that it will boost retail price tags on its passenger cars by an average of 500-dollars because of increasing costs of steel and rubber.

2. General Motors is raising its new car prices. The average increase is 500-dollars. G-M says it has to charge more because steel and rubber costs are up.

If you think the first lead is the better broadcast news lead, turn to page 13.

If you think the second lead is better, turn to page 14.

So, you think the one long sentence is the better broadcast style lead? Read it out loud.

General Motors Corporation has announced that it will boost retail price tags on its passenger cars by an average of 500-dollars because of increasing costs of steel and rubber.

It's quite a mouthful, don't you think? And maybe just a little awkward? Is it the way you would tell it to a friend? Would you really say, "Hey Jack, have you heard? General Motors Corporation has announced that it will boost retail price tags on its passenger cars by an average of $500 because of increasing costs of steel and rubber"?

You'd more likely say, "Hey Jack, have you heard? General Motors has raised its new car prices. The average increase is $500. Five hundred dollars . . . can you believe it? Everything is going up these days. I wish the price of steel and rubber hadn't gone up."

Of course, you can't always write the story exactly as you would tell it to a friend, but you can come close. Try to make your leads as conversational as possible. Remember *sound* is important. You're trying to write a lead that will *sound* good to the listeners and that will be easy for them to understand.

Turn to page 14 and try two more leads.

Nice going. You picked the right one. The one long sentence has been broken up into three short, crisp sentences. Yet the flow is still there. It's easier to understand this way, and it *sounds* better. Remember, *sound* is important. Both leads are acceptable, but the meaning is clearer in the second one, and it's a lot easier on the ear.

Choose a Lead #2

Record or read the next two leads out loud and decide which one is the better broadcast news lead.

1. The Teamsters walkout continues at five major supermarket warehouses. Union members have decided to ignore their union leaders and a court order.

2. Ignoring their union leaders and a court order, Teamsters members have continued their walkout at five major supermarket warehouses.

If you think the first lead is better broadcast style, turn to page 15.

If you think the second lead is better, turn to page 16.

All right. You're doing fine. The first lead is definitely the better of the two. It gives the important elements first—"the walkout is continuing." The two-sentence form is short and sweet. It's easy on the ear, simple, clear, direct, and understandable. Keep up the good work.

Choose a Lead #3

Record or read the next two leads out loud.

1.   The F-B-I is looking for the business agent of Aerocraft Leasing Company. One of the company's planes crashed in a Miami neighborhood last night killing eight people, and F-B-I officials think the business agent could have prevented the crash.

2.   The business agent for the Aerocraft Leasing Company, the operators of a plane that crashed in a Miami neighborhood last night and killed eight people, is being sought by the F-B-I today because bureau officials think he could have prevented the crash.

If you think the first lead is the better one, turn to page 17.

If you think the second lead is better, turn to page 18.

Bad choice. Remember, it's not a good idea to start a sentence with a descriptive clause or phrase. That's what happened here. "Ignoring their union leaders and a court order" is a phrase. If you hit the listeners with something like this right at the start of the story, they won't know what you're talking about. What group is ignoring its union leaders and a court order?

While the listeners are wondering, they'll probably miss the name of the union. Let the listeners in on WHO is doing WHAT before you get into the circumstances.

Remember, you're trying to lead the listeners by the ear through your story, so give them a break. Tell them what you know in a way they'll be able to understand. Take the time to think how you would tell the story to a friend. Would you really say, "Jill, have you heard? Ignoring their union leaders and a court order, Teamsters members have continued their walkout at five major supermarket warehouses"?

You'd probably say something like "the Teamsters walkout is still going on at those five supermarket warehouses. Union leaders have told them to stop and so has the court, but they're still striking."

Now, turn back to page 15 and record or read the next two leads out loud. Choose the one that *sounds* more natural and conversational to you.

Correct. The first lead is the better of the two. It's clearer, more listenable, and far more understandable than the second one.

Choose a Lead #4

Record or read the next two leads out loud.

1.   Kevin Carlson and Mollie Smith were married this morning in Chicago by their U-S Army recruiting officer, who also is an ordained Methodist minister.

2.   An unusual wedding in Chicago this morning. Kevin Carlson and Mollie Smith were married by their U-S Army recruiting officer. The recruiter is also a Methodist minister, so everything's legal.

If you think the first lead is better, turn to page 19.

If you think the second lead is better, turn to page 20.

No. Sorry. The second lead is really awful. It's not even an acceptable newspaper lead. Too much information is crowded into one long sentence. Didn't you get a little confused when you were listening to it on tape or saying it out loud?

The long clause that helps describe the aircraft company really breaks up the continuity of the sentence. Remember, the simple subject–verb–object sentence is the best one to use. It's clear, direct, and understandable.

Go back and take another look at the two leads again. Try starting each lead with "Hey Jack, have you heard?" See which one *sounds* better to you.

You'll see that the first lead is the better broadcast news style lead. It's more natural—more conversational. Remember, think the way you talk and write the way you talk.

After you've looked over the leads again, record or read the two leads on page 17 out loud.

This one's a little tricky, but you should have been able to decide which lead was the better one by using that good old "Hey Jill" formula. Go back and try putting a "Hey Jill, guess what . . . ?" at the beginning of each lead. See which one *sounds* more natural—more like what you'd really say.

One extra piece of advice. It's not a good idea to start out a broadcast news story with an unknown name like Kevin Carlson. Too many listeners will miss it. Try to ease listeners into a name. Tease the listeners' curiosity first before hitting them with the names of the people involved.

Well-known names like those of your mayor, governor, U.S. senators, the president, professional athletes, or movie stars might be okay to put right at the beginning of the story—because people will recognize the names of celebrities—but little-known or completely unknown names should be used after you've piqued the listeners' attention.

Go back and reread the two leads on the Army wedding. Then turn to page 20.

Good choice. The second lead is the better one for broadcast news. The first sentence sets the listeners up for the information in the second and third sentences.

"An unusual wedding in Chicago this morning." The sentence sets the tone for the story. It tells the listeners what the story is going to be about. It characterizes the story, and that's what a lead is supposed to do.

Remember, the lead is somewhat like a newspaper headline. It should NOT be written in "headlinese," but it should clue listeners in to what is coming up and it should attract the listeners' attention.

Try to write leads that would logically follow the opening, "Hey, did you hear?" If you can do that and make it *sound* natural and real, you're on your way to mastering the art of broadcast newswriting.

We're going to leave leads for a while and go on to some other elements of broadcast newswriting, but later we'll come back and give you a shot at writing some leads of your own.

- ## NAMES AND TITLES

What's in a Name?

Just about every story you'll write will have at least one name in it. Most of the time there will be several names. Be sure to get all of the names correct—spelling and pronunciation.

Nothing shoots down a broadcaster's credibility more than botching up somebody's name. When listeners hear a name mispronounced—or worse, the wrong name—they begin to wonder how much of the rest of the information is wrong, too. In addition, you offend news sources when their names are mispronounced. They'll likely think twice about dealing with you and your station again.

Take the time to check the names of people making news. When they're local, you can call them up and ask about the correct spelling and pronunciation of their names. When they're national figures, sometimes the wire services will have a name advisory you can check. You can also call the local branch of the agency or organization that the person represents.

Remember to ask around the newsroom, too. You never know what some of your fellow workers might know unless you ask.

Sometimes you'll get stuck on the correct way to pronounce a word. Don't forget that the dictionary is a good source.

Be sure to include a pronunciation guide for difficult names, places, and words. The guides should be placed in parentheses above the correctly spelled name or word. The syllable in all capitals is the emphasized syllable.

        (KRISH-oh-man)
Example: Alex Chriseoman

        (ihn-SAY-shuh-bull)
Example: insatiable

A good source for writing pronunciation guides is the *United Press International Broadcast Stylebook*. UPI guidelines are in the Appendix.

Who Was That?

Names provide other problems for the broadcast newswriter. Listeners aren't always paying close attention to what the newscaster is saying, so if you start a story with a relatively unknown name, a lot of listeners will miss it.

Give the half-listening listeners a break. Give them a little hint that you're going to throw a name at them. Start with the person's title if he has one, or give a little information about why a little-known person is suddenly in the news.

Example (poor): Peter Jones of Midcity won the World Kissing Championship last night. He said it was

the most fun he'd ever had.

Example (better): A Midcity man won the World Kissing Championship last night. Peter Jones said it

was the most fun he'd ever had.

The second example is called *delayed identification*. It's a technique used quite often in broadcast newswriting. It's a good way to help your listeners catch a person's name.

In the above example, if Peter Jones had a title, you could start with it.

Example: State Senator Peter Jones won the World Kissing Championship last night.

Example: Councilman Peter Jones won the World Kissing Championship last night.

If Peter Jones is very well known it would be okay to start with his name because listeners would recognize it and it would serve to arouse their interest. But when the name is not very well known, or not known at all, start with a title or what has made the name newsworthy.

When a person is well known because of the position he or she holds, it's usually okay to use the person's title with the last name only, leaving out the first name.

Example: Governor Hernandez

Example: Senator Heftel

Example: Mayor Anderson

Example: President Clinton

If it *sounds* okay to leave out the first name, leave it out. If it *sounds* better to leave the first name in, leave it in. Let your ear be your guide. Remember, though, except for well-known people, ALWAYS include full first and last name when you use a person's title.

Endless Titles

Some titles can get fairly long and involved. When you run into one of these, try to shorten or break it up into smaller parts so you won't have to stick all of it in front of the person's name.

Example (poor): The vice-president of the Midcity Women for the Protection and Enhancement of the Female Image on Television, Lori McFadden, says her group will sponsor an "Awareness Fair" next Friday. She says more than 10-thousand women will take part.

Example (better): The vice-president of a local women's organization says her group will sponsor an "Awareness Fair" next Friday. Lori McFadden, of the Midcity Women for the Protection and Enhancement of the Female Image of Television, says more than 10-thousand women will take part.

You can probably come up with other ways of handling long, awkward titles. The important thing is to be sure to break up mouthful titles into digestible pieces.

First Names First

When you use any name, except that of a well-known government official, the initial reference should include both the person's first and last names. Later references should be made using only the person's last name. This rule applies to both men and women.

Example: Doctor Sharon Ishida is the new president of the Midcity Unified School District Board of

Education. Ishida replaces Professor Donald Sneed.

Eliminate the Middleman

A middle name or initial is rarely used in broadcast newswriting unless the name or initial has become associated with a person.

Examples: J. Edgar Hoover

P. T. Barnum

J. Paul Getty

H. Ross Perot

Edward R. Murrow

Edward G. Robinson

Billie Jean King

Try your hand at the name game on the next page.

The Name Game

Using the correct broadcast news style, where would you put the person's name in the following sentences? Check the appropriate blank.

A. The president of Nuvo Motors, Kenneth Warren, says his company is going out of business.

Where it is ___   Before the title ___   Leave it out ___

B. Maria Rodriquez, a Midcity housewife, has been elected president of the National Homemakers Association.

Where it is ___   After the title ___   Leave it out ___

C. Karen Murphy, the newly elected chairperson of the Midcity Realtor's Association, will speak at the luncheon.

Where it is ___   After the title ___   Leave it out ___

D. The chairman of the Senate Investigating Committee on Crime, Violence, Perversion, Obscenity, and Pornography, Joel Davis, is being investigated for income tax evasion.

Where it is ___   Before the title ___   Leave it out ___

E. The governor of Western New Zealand, Leonard Theodore, will visit the United States in late April.

Where it is ___   Before the title ___   Leave it out ___

F. Ruby Thybo, the director of the Midcity Friends of Cats Society, is looking for volunteers.

Where it is ___   After the title ___   Leave it out ___

Check your answers on the next page.

Answers to the Name Game

A. Where it is. The title is short enough to come before the name.

B. After the title. Remember, titles always come before the name if they're not extremely long and involved. This one is short enough to come before the name.

C. After the title. This title is getting close to being too long, but it's not quite long enough, so put it before the name.

D. Before the title. This title is really too long to stick in front of the name. You could break it up by writing, "Senator Joel Davis, who is the chairman of the Senate Investigating Committee on Crime. . . ." Or you might write, "Senator Joel Davis is being investigated for income tax evasion. He's the chairman of the Senate Investigating Committee on Crime. . . ." However you do it, the important thing is to come up with a way of breaking up long, involved, awkward titles.

E. Leave it out. Is his name really that important? Does it add anything to the story? Why not use just the title only in the first sentence and use the name later in the story?

F. After the title. Give the listeners a break. You don't want them to miss the name of such a warm-hearted woman, do you? Put the title first so the listeners can anticipate the name.

If you missed more than two, you might want to go back and reread the section on titles. After you've done that, or if you missed two or less, go on to the next page.

- ## IDENTIFICATION

   ### Identification Please

   Using titles is a good way to help identify people. Titles help distinguish Councilman Joe Smith from Professor Joe Smith, Reporter Joe Smith, Police Officer Joe Smith, Fire Fighter Joe Smith, and all the other Joe Smiths in your community. You want to be as specific in identifying people as possible.

   You don't want to just say, "Joe Smith has been convicted of murder," when it's Professor Joe Smith who's been convicted. If you don't include the title—one of the things that makes one Joe Smith different from the other Joe Smiths—your listeners might get confused. That not only could be embarrassing for all the innocent Joe Smiths, but it could lead to a libel suit against you and your station.

- ## ADDRESSES

   ### Home Sweet Home

   Try to find out the titles of people in the news and use them in your stories. When you can't get a person's title, it's a good idea to include his address to help identify him.

   Example: Joe Smith, who lives at 29-83 Dove Avenue, is the new spokesperson.

   Example: Joe Smith, of 29-83 Dove Avenue, is the new spokesperson.

   When you include an address, it lets your listeners know it's the Joe Smith who lives at 2983 Dove Avenue who is involved and NOT the Joe Smith who lives at 6745 Mercer Drive.

   Whenever you include an address, use the "who lives at" or the "of" prior to the street numbers and name. It *sounds* more conversational.

   You don't have to include addresses for all of the people in every story, but when specific identification is required—as in a crime story, an accident, or a trial—or when you don't have a title for the person, it's a good idea to give the address.

   You don't always have to give all the specifics of the address. You can give the part of town, the street name, or a general block number. This technique helps protect a person's privacy.

   Example: Joe Smith, of East Midcity, . . .

   Example: Joe Smith, of Mercer Drive, . . .

   Example: Joe Smith, of the 67-hundred block of Mercer Drive, . . .

- ## AGES

   ### Age Gracefully

   Many broadcast newswriters like to use a person's age as part of the identification process. This practice can get a bit tedious, especially if your story has three or four names in it.

   Include a person's age only if it is significant to the story or if you have no other means of identifying him. You'd probably want to mention a person's age if he were unusually young or old to be involved in whatever he's involved in, but using a person's age merely for identification purposes is not a good practice.

If you have a person's title and/or address, why use his age, too? When you have nothing you can use for identification except his age, then use it.

When you do need to use someone's age, use it with the first and last name and write it in one of the following ways:

Example: 47-year-old Arthur Lord

Example: Arthur Lord, who is 47-years-old, . . .

Example: Arthur Lord died today. He was 47-years-old.

NEVER place an age after a name, as is often done in newspapers, and NEVER use a person's age with his last name only.

Example (poor): Arthur Lord, 47, . . .

Example (poor): the 47-year-old Lord

It is acceptable to use a person's age in connection with his title or with what has made him newsworthy. In such cases, you might delay the person's name until the next sentence.

Example: A 29-year-old Midcity construction worker won 40-million-dollars in the state lottery last night.

Stan Davis plans to keep on working, though.

Example: A five-year-old girl died this morning in a freak accident. Lisa Lynn Hunt fell off a swing and

broke her neck.

• ATTRIBUTION

Who Says So?

Attribution is the "who says so" in broadcast news stories. It's the source of the information. You report attribution just as you do in normal speech. Stop and think about how you tell a story to a friend.

Example: Jerry said we ought to go to the movies. But Gayle said she'd rather grab a burger. Mark said

he wanted pizza. Finally, Courtney said we should go to "Nick's Place," so that's what we did.

See how all the attribution—the who says so—is always at the beginning, before what was said. That's the way attribution is reported in broadcast newswriting—at the beginning—NOT dangling at the end of a sentence or plopped in the middle of a sentence as you've seen in newspapers.

Example (poor): "I've discovered a cure for cancer and it really works," Doctor Beverly Atwater said today.

Example (poor): "I've discovered a cure for cancer," Doctor Beverly Atwater said today, "and it really works."

Example (better): Doctor Beverly Atwater says she's discovered a cure for cancer that really works.

Don't you think the last sentence *sounds* better and more natural with the attribution at the beginning? Besides, with the attribution at the beginning of the sentence, your listeners will know it's Dr. Beverly Atwater and not the newscaster who's discovered a cure for cancer.

It's important to let listeners know right at the start who says what. There are times in broadcast newswriting when attribution is delayed, but at this stage in your career as a broadcast newswriter, place attribution at the beginning of sentences—who says so BEFORE what is said.

Try your hand at Attribution Test #1 on the next page.

Attribution Test #1

Indicate where you would put the attribution in the following sentences. Check your answers on the next page.

A. Professor Jerry Nelson says the time has come for students to revolt.

   Where it is ___   End ___   Middle ___

B. "Poverty is only a state of mind," Susan Lynn said.

   Where it is ___   Beginning ___   Middle ___

C. Christmas, Ebenezer Scrooge says, is for humbugs.

   Where it is ___   Beginning ___   End ___

D. "Nothing excites my husband more than a good war movie," Joyce Boyd said.

   Where it is ___   Beginning ___   Middle ___

E. "Midcity is America's finest city," Councilwoman Anita Liang said.

   Where it is ___   Beginning ___   Middle ___

F. Professor Tim Wulfemeyer says this learning experience for beginning broadcast newswriters is fantastic.

   Where it is ___   End ___   Middle ___

G. We need a stronger military force, General Willard Williams reported, because the Chinese are developing a new missile.

   Where it is ___   Beginning ___   End ___

Answers to Attribution Test #1

A. Where it is.

B. Beginning.

C. Beginning.

D. Beginning.

E. Beginning.

F. Where it is.

G. Beginning.

All the attributions should be put at the beginning of the sentences. Remember, the "who says so" in broadcast news comes before what was said.

If you didn't get *all* the attributions at the beginning of each sentence, you should go back and reread the section on attribution.

Say It with *Says*

There seems to be a perpetual contest going on in broadcast newswriting to see who can come up with the most synonyms for *says*. All you have to do is check the dictionary and you'll find lots of words that can be used for attribution.

Examples: declares, discloses, points out, demands, states, maintains, remarks, claims, exclaims, proclaims, insists

What's wrong with *says* or *said*? You don't have to use a different word each time you want to attribute something to somebody. *Claims, insists, discloses,* and all the rest have a slight tinge of editorial comment to them.

Reports is the least offensive of all the synonyms for *says,* so if you feel the need to vary your words of attribution from time to time, use *reports. According to* is another acceptable alternative. Leave all the others to the paperback writers.

If a person promises or asks something, you can report that he *promises* or *asks* it. But if a person merely makes a statement—just says something—use *says*. NEVER use *stated*. It sounds too formal and unnatural.

• REPETITION

Repeat, Repeat, Repeat

Don't be afraid to repeat words. If the word is the *right* word, don't hesitate to use it—more than once, twice, or even three times. If the word fits, write it.

Don't fall into the trap that many sportswriters do. No team ever *beats* or *defeats* another team any more. It *humbles, nips, blasts, bombs, pounds, rips, cages, knifes, trounces, blanks, squashes, trips, corrals,* or *bashes* the other team.

You can take color and variety too far in your writing. Use the natural words, the conversational words. You don't always have to be looking up synonyms to be a good writer. Use the words that you would use if you were telling your story to a friend.

● QUOTES

Quotable Quotes

Direct quotes—the speaker's *exact* words—are a little hard to handle in broadcast newswriting. Quotation marks don't do much good. They might tell the newscaster to change the inflection in his voice a little, but that's about it.

When you really want the listeners to know that the words are the speaker's *exact* words, there are several ways you can do it. Whatever you do, NEVER use the old "quote, unquote" method. It *sounds* too stiff and formal.

Example (poor): Frank Merriwell says . . . quote . . . "Football builds men" . . . unquote.

If you want your listeners to know that the words are the speaker's *exact* words, you can use "quoting from his exact words," "and we're quoting him," "as he put it," "as she expressed it," or "and these are his words."

Example: Frank Merriwell said . . . and we're quoting him . . . "Football builds men."

Example: Senator Steinberg says . . . and these are his exact words . . . "Anybody making more than 100-thousand-dollars a year should have to pay extra income tax."

Example: Police Chief Mario Soto said . . . and this is the way he put it . . . "Organized crime controls all the local bars."

There are other ways of introducing direct quotations, but the important thing is to make sure your listeners know the words are the speaker's and not yours. Listeners can't see the quotation marks in your copy, so you have to come up with another way to let them know.

By all means, if you're going to quote somebody's *exact* words, quote the *exact* words. Quote full sentences, not parts or bits and pieces.

Example (poor): Igor Kranak said he never dreamed life could be . . . what he called . . . "such a wonderful merry-go-round."

Example (better): Igor Kranak said . . . and this is the way he expressed it . . . "I never dreamed life could be such a wonderful merry-go-round."

When you come across a long quotation, there's the problem of getting out of it—of letting the listeners know you're through quoting a speaker. Some ways to do it are:

Example: That's what (so and so) said about (whatever).

Example: Those were (so and so's) exact words.

Example: That's the way (so and so) put it.

Example: Anna Poynter said . . . and we're quoting her . . . "I've never seen anything so horrible. The flames were everywhere. I tried to get into the house, but it was no use. I just couldn't make it. I wish I'd never let Edgar smoke in bed. If I would have made him quit, he'd still be alive." That's what Anna Poynter said about the fire that killed her husband and destroyed her home early this morning.

Close but No Cigar

You can see how direct quotes are difficult and awkward to handle. Unless the *exact* words are so colorful or are so unique as to warrant being quoted exactly, avoid using direct quotations.

Paraphrase and use the form, "So and so says such and such." You can keep the essence of what a speaker said without having to quote him exactly. If the exact wording of the quote is not all that important, unusual, descriptive, or colorful, use an indirect quote—a paraphrase.

Those last direct quotes used as examples can be written as indirect quotes very easily.

Example: Frank Merriwell says football builds men.

Example: Senator Steinberg says anybody making more than 100-thousand-dollars a year should have to pay extra income tax.

Example: Police Chief Mario Soto says organized crime controls all the local bars.

Example: Anna Poynter said she'd never seen anything so horrible. She said she tried to get into the house, but the flames were everywhere. She said if she'd made her husband Edgar stop smoking in bed, he'd still be alive.

Usually you don't lose anything by paraphrasing. In fact, sometimes you can gain clarity and leave out needless words.

Quotations Test

Rewrite each of the following sentences twice: First as a direct quote—making sure listeners will know the words are the speaker's exact words—and second as a paraphrased quote. Check your rewrites on the next page.

1. "I think college basketball is becoming too commercialized," Midcity Athletic Director Mark Wulf said.

DIRECT QUOTE:

PARAPHRASED QUOTE:

2. "I have decided to run for Governor," State Senator Sharon Kim announced today, "because this state needs new leadership. For too many years we've been too content with old methods and old solutions, but now we need new methods and new solutions to meet the challenges ahead."

DIRECT QUOTE:

PARAPHRASED QUOTE:

Answers to Quotations Test

1. **Direct quote:**

Midcity Athletic Director Mark Wulf says . . . and these are his exact words . . . college basketball is becoming too commercialized.

2. **Direct quote:**

State Senator Sharon Kim said today . . . and we're quoting her exactly . . . I've decided to run for Governor, because this state needs new leadership. For too many years we've been too content with old methods and old solutions, but now we need new methods and new solutions to meet the challenges ahead.

Any of the "exact words" phrases would be okay to use. The important thing is to let your listeners know that the words are the exact words the source used.

1. **Indirect quote:**

Midcity University Athletic Director Mark Wulf says college basketball is becoming too commercialized.

2. **Indirect quote:**

State Senator Sharon Kim says she's going to run for governor. She says the state needs new leadership, because for too long we've been using old methods and solutions to deal with our problems. Kim says we need new methods and solutions to deal with the challenges of the future.

There are other ways you could have handled the indirect quotes, but see how indirect quotes can cut down excess wording? They are usually clearer too, so use them most of the time in your broadcast newswriting.

● FACTS OR OPINION?

To Attribute or Not To Attribute

Sometimes it's hard to know whether or not to attribute a statement or some piece of information. Generally, *facts* DO NOT need attribution, but *opinions* DO need attribution. When in doubt, however, let the listeners know where you got your information.

Be sure to include attribution whenever a statement or piece of information:

1. Implies blame.

2. Hasn't been proven to be true.

3. Might be controversial.

4. Might be questionable.

Keep these "attribution musts" in mind as you take the self-test on the next page.

Attribution Test #2

Indicate whether attribution is needed in the following sentences.

A. A hurricane ripped across Florida this morning.

   Needed ___   Not Needed ___

B. Mayor Shelley should be recalled.

   Needed ___   Not Needed___

C. The Minnesota Vikings are the best team in professional football.

   Needed ___   Not Needed ___

D. A jumbo jet has crashed at the Midcity Municipal Airport.

   Needed ___   Not Needed ___

E. Lots of heated discussion at the Board of Education meeting this afternoon.

   Needed ___   Not Needed ___

F. The oil companies create gasoline shortages so they can make higher profits.

   Needed ___   Not Needed ___

G. The price of milk is up again.

   Needed ___   Not Needed ___

H. If the bill passes, it will mean the end to freedom of speech.

   Needed ___   Not Needed ___

I. The Tigers defeated the Yankees 4-to-3.

   Needed ___   Not Needed ___

Check your answers on the next page.

Answers to Attribution Test #2

A. Not needed. Fact. Who would dispute it?

B. Needed. Opinion. Listeners will want to know who wants to recall the mayor.

C. Needed. Opinion. Controversial and questionable. Plenty of people would dispute it, too.

D. Not needed. Fact.

E. Not needed. This is a fact—at least as the reporter sees it. He or she attended the meeting and determined it to be true. If you checked "Needed," you really aren't wrong though. Some would argue that this type of statement should have attribution. Actually, very often the question of whether or not to attribute a statement boils down to judgment. Things aren't always clear cut. Use your best judgment, but keep in mind that facts DO NOT need attribution and opinions DO need attribution.

F. Needed. Opinion. Statement implies blame and certainly would be disputed.

G. Not needed. Fact.

H. Needed. Opinion. It's questionable, controversial, and probably isn't true.

I. Not needed. Fact.

If you missed more than one, you should reread the section on attribution. After you finish checking over the attribution section, or if you missed one or none of the attribution questions, proceed to the next page.

• AIDING THE LISTENERS

Half-Listening Listeners

The half-listening listener is one of the facts of life in broadcasting, especially broadcast news. Rarely does anyone listen to the radio or watch the news on television without a number of distractions. Kids are fighting or talking loudly; the dog is barking; a roommate, husband, wife, boyfriend, girlfriend, or some member of the family is doing something or saying something.

A person could be driving, eating, studying, doing housework, preparing food, working on a project, reading, dreaming, or just thinking about something else besides listening to the news that's coming from the radio or the television.

As a newswriter, you have to try to overcome these distractions and get the news to your listeners, no matter how preoccupied or inattentive they may be. We've already talked about some ways to gain the listeners' attention by writing crisp, snappy leads and giving a person's title and the attribution at the beginning of the sentence.

There are some other ways that you can give the half-listening listeners a break. You can *repeat* the extremely significant parts of stories toward the end so listeners who missed them the first time can get them the second time around.

You can mention the place where the big fire has destroyed thousands of trees near the end of the story as well as at the beginning. Repetition has a place in broadcast news if the information deserves more than one mention.

Another way to help the half-listening listeners is to avoid the words *former* and *latter*. Your listeners aren't going to remember who was mentioned first and who was mentioned second. Besides, listeners can't go back and relisten for something they missed or forgot as readers can go back and reread. Instead of *former* and *latter*, just mention again the last names of the people involved.

Example (poor): The judge decided in favor of Maxwell Marlowe and Jacob Stein. The former collected

10-thousand-dollars and the latter picked up eight-thousand.

Example (better): The judge decided in favor of Maxwell Marlowe and Jacob Stein. Marlowe collected

10-thousand-dollars and Stein picked up eight-thousand.

Remember, try to give your listeners a break. They have a lot of distractions, but they still want to get the news. It's your job to get it to them.

• CONTRACTIONS

Contractions Can't Hurt

Contractions are good for what ails so much of broadcast newswriting style—stiffness and formality. How often do you say, "Jill *did not* want to go skiing"? Never? You'd probably say, "Jill *didn't* want to go skiing."

Don't be afraid to use contractions. You do all the time in your everyday speech, so why not use them in your broadcast news copy? They sound natural and conversational, so use them when they're appropriate.

There are times when you should NOT use contractions. One is when you want emphasis.

Example: Governor Atkin says he will NOT call in the National Guard.

When you want that *not* to come through loud and clear, write it in. Don't cover it up by using *won't*. Make it stand out.

Another time you might not want to use contractions is when the severity or formality of the situation dictates a more formal communication style. For instance, in reporting a major disaster, it would be better to say "The number of deaths has NOT been determined," rather than "The number of deaths hasn't been determined."

Use your own judgment, but remember—in most cases it *sounds* better to say *didn't* instead of *did not, shouldn't* instead of *should not, won't* instead of *will not, we'll* instead of *we will,* and *they're* instead of *they are.*

Some other contractions you might use are

haven't **for** have not	isn't **for** is not
couldn't **for** could not	wasn't **for** was not
you're **for** you are	it's **for** it is
can't **for** cannot	they'll **for** they will
aren't **for** are not	doesn't **for** does not

• PRONOUNS

Who's He?

Using personal pronouns is a good way to humanize your copy. Use *we, us, our, they, you, he, she, it* wherever you can. But remember, whenever you use a personal pronoun, be sure it refers to the appropriate noun—the one you're talking about.

Example (poor): Professor Marvin Jones helped Doctor George Langly with the experiment. He's from Iowa State University.

Who is "he" in the example? Is it Jones or Langly? It's hard to tell from the way it's written. You can imagine the poor listeners when they hear something like this. They just shake their heads and wonder, "Who's he?"

Pronouns usually refer to the last noun used in a sentence or paragraph. In the example, that would mean the "he" refers to George Langly, but is that what you want? More than likely the "he" is supposed to refer to Marvin Jones. The point is, if you want to avoid confusion and misunderstanding, be careful when you use personal pronouns. Make sure they refer to the intended noun—the one you want.

Example: Professor Marvin Jones helped Doctor George Langly with the experiment. Jones is from Iowa State University.

You Is Us

Another good way to humanize your copy is to use *we* and *us* and *our* instead of *you* and *your.* As a newswriter, you are a part of the community, not some impartial observer. News that affects your listeners affects you, too.

Example (poor): *Your* electric bills will be going up soon.

Example (better): *Our* electric bills will be going up soon.

Example (poor): *You're* in for a cold winter.

Example (better): *We're* in for a cold winter.

Let your listeners know you feel like an active member of the community. It will improve your credibility and popularity, plus it will help you communicate better.

• VERB TENSE

Now Is the Time

Radio and television are the media of the moment. They are the "what's happening now" media. You should use the present tense of verbs or the present perfect tense whenever you can to emphasize this sense of immediacy.

Use *says* instead of *said, has reported* instead of *reported*. This doesn't mean that you should abandon the past tense altogether, but use it sparingly to describe things that have taken place in the fairly distant past.

Example: We *reported* last week that the price of eggs *was going* up . . . but now it *looks* as if we *had*

our facts scrambled.

You probably noticed the mixing of verb tenses in the example. That's perfectly okay to do in broadcast newswriting. You can vary verb tenses in your sentences as long as the sentences make sense. Varying verb tenses can help break up monotony.

Example: The Defense Department *has issued* a warning to Iraq. It *says* if the Iraqis *don't pull out* of

Kuwait, the U-S *will have to invade* Baghdad. Iraqi leaders *had* no comment.

As long as the sentence *sounds* right, you're okay. Just make sure that when the sentence is read out loud, it makes sense.

• TIME ELEMENTS

Timely Time

When you use the past or future tense, you'll probably want to include the time element of the story—WHEN the story happened or WHEN it will happen. WHEN the action happened or will happen is often an important element, but you don't want to say "today" in every story. You'll bore your listeners and yourself.

Try to be specific in your use of time. Use *this morning, this afternoon, this evening, minutes ago, just before we came on the air,* or whatever you can to convey as closely as possible the exact time of the event.

Natural Time

Avoid the awkward placement of the time element in the sentence. Write it in where it *sounds* most natural. Usually, it's best to place the time element right before or after the verb. It's often placed at the end of the sentence. If you put it at the beginning of the sentence, you give added emphasis to it.

Example (poor): U-S Treasurer Doris Williams this morning resigned after a meeting with her lawyer.

Example (better): U-S Treasurer Doris Williams resigned this morning after a meeting with her lawyer.

Example (better): This morning U-S Treasurer Doris Williams resigned after a meeting with her lawyer.

Example (better): U-S Treasurer Doris Williams resigned after a meeting with her lawyer this morning.

A time element often sounds awkward when it's used with a present tense or present perfect tense verb, but a time element does flow naturally out of a past tense or future tense verb.

Example (poor): Joe Spar *says* this morning that he's giving up boxing.

Example (better): Joe Spar *said* this morning that he's giving up boxing.

As with so much else in broadcast newswriting, when it comes to placing the time element in the sentence, let your ear be your guide.

• VERB VOICE

Action Please

Another thing to remember when you're selecting a verb is to use the active voice instead of the passive voice. A good, strong active verb will usually get across your meaning better than a passive verb.

Example (poor): The dog *was bitten* by the man.

Example (better): The man *bit* the dog.

Example (poor): Fire officials say the fire *was caused* by a short circuit.

Example (better): Fire officials say a short circuit *caused* the fire.

Example (poor): Midcity University *has been given* a five-million-dollar grant by the Albert Parvin Foundation.

Example(better): The Albert Parvin Foundation *has given* a five-million-dollar grant to Midcity University.

You can use the passive voice sometimes, but keep it to a minimum. It slows down the pace of your story and robs it of life and pep. Most of the time use the simple declarative sentence (subject-verb-object). It's the best.

The rewriting test on the next page gives you an opportunity to practice correct broadcast newswriting.

• REWRITING

Rewriting Test

Here's a chance for you to see how well you've understood the sections covering contractions, personal pronouns, verb tenses, verb voices, and time elements. Rewrite each of the following sentences using correct broadcast news style.

A. State Senator James Miller today has decided to sue columnist George Wilson. He has accused him of lying.

B. Councilwoman Marilyn Munson said she has not accepted campaign contributions today, because she is not sure whether they are appropriate.

C. The winning run was driven in by Reggie Norton.

D. Looks as if you will be paying more for light bulbs soon.

E. The final two spots went to Mary Flint and Mike Harrison. The former is a native of Harrisburg, Pennsylvania, and the latter is from Flintsville, Iowa.

F. This afternoon fire has destroyed the Mueller Antiques store on Broadway. The fire was caused by faulty wiring, said fire officials.

Check your answers on the next page.

Answers to Rewriting Test

A. **Rewrite:** State Senator James Miller has decided to sue columnist George Wilson. Miller has accused Wilson of lying.

Drop *today*. Replace *he* with *Miller* and *him* with *Wilson*. Remember, keep your personal pronouns straight and avoid the awkward and needless use of a time element.

B. **Rewrite:** Councilwoman Marilyn Munson says she hasn't accepted campaign contributions, because she's not sure they're appropriate.

Change *said* to *says*. Change *has not* to *hasn't*. Change *she is* to *she's*. Change *they are* to *they're*. Drop *today*. Remember, use the present tense of verbs and contractions whenever possible. Plus, be sure to place the time element where it sounds most natural and if you don't need a time element, drop it.

C. **Rewrite:** Reggie Norton drove in the winning run.

Change the passive verb *was driven in* to the active verb *drove in*. Remember, use active verbs whenever possible. They add pep to your sentences.

D. **Rewrite:** Looks as if we'll be paying more for light bulbs soon.

Change *you will* to *we'll*. Use contractions, plus remember that you're in the same boat as your listeners. You is us, they are we, and your is our.

E. **Rewrite:** The final two spots have gone to Mary Flint and Mike Harrison. Flint is from Harrisburg, Pennsylvania, and Harrison is from Flintsville, Iowa.

Change the past tense *went* to the present perfect tense *have gone*. It makes the copy sound a bit more timely. Replace *former* with *Flint* and *latter* with *Harrison*. Remember, NEVER use *former* and *latter*. Your listeners can't go back and find out who was the former and who was the latter. Use the persons' names again. You'll be helping the half-listening listeners.

F. **Rewrite:** Fire destroyed the Mueller Antiques store on Broadway this afternoon. Fire officials say faulty wiring caused the fire.

Change *has destroyed* to *destroyed*. Move time element to end of sentence. Move attribution to beginning of sentence. Make second sentence active voice by changing *was caused* to *caused* and making *faulty wiring* the subject of the sentence. Remember, place time elements where they sound the most natural and avoid the use of time elements with the present perfect tense of verbs. In addition, keep your sentences in the ACTIVE voice whenever you can.

If you missed three or more of the changes, you'd better go back and reread the sections. You need to master all of the concepts to be an effective broadcast newswriter.

After you reread the sections, or if you missed less than three, go on to the next page.

• ABBREVIATIONS

What Does T-H-A-T Stand For?

The use of abbreviations in broadcast newswriting can generally be summed up in three words: don't use them. Give the person who is going to be reading your copy on the air a little consideration. He or she might have trouble translating an abbreviation into words.

You yourself might even forget if you're reading your own copy on the air. Play it safe. SPELL OUT words so they look the way you want them to be read. Never abbreviate the names of states, countries, days of the week, months, government titles, religious titles, military titles, address designations, or the words *junior* or *senior*.

Some abbreviations, such as Mr. and Mrs. and U.S., are so recognizable they're safe to use, but generally it's best to write out the word.

Examples (poor): Calif., N.Z., Wed., Nov., Gov., Rev., Sgt., St., Dr., Blvd.

Examples (better): California, New Zealand, Wednesday, November, Governor, Reverend, Sergeant,

Street, Drive, Boulevard

Organized Organizations

The names of most organizations should be written out completely the first time they appear in a story. Every additional reference can be made with the initials or a shortened version of the name.

Example: People Opposed to Pornography . . . known as POP . . . is at it again. POP members are

burning all the dirty books they can find.

The same method can be used even if the group's name doesn't reduce to a neat acronym like POP.

Example: The Iowa Highway Patrol is on the lookout for speeders. The I-H-P says it's starting a new

"get-tough" policy.

Some groups have become so well known by their abbreviated names that it's okay to use them without giving the full name first.

Example: North Atlantic Treaty Organization is NATO.

Example: National Aeronautics and Space Administration is NASA.

There are others, but make sure you're not taking too much for granted by using the abbreviated form of an organization's name. When in doubt, give the full name of the organization the first time you mention it in a story.

A R-O-S-E Is Not a ROSE

You might have noticed the hyphens between I-H-P and the lack of hyphens between NASA. In broadcast newswriting you use hyphens between letters and numbers that you want pronounced separately.

Example: Capitalize and place hyphens between U-N, U-S, F-B-I, I-O-U, T-N-T, C-I-A, C-B-S, N-B-C,

W-O-I-T-V, G-O-P, N-double-A-C-P.

Example: The phone number is 2-9-2-1-7-5-9.

Example: The phone number is 2-9-2-17-59.

Example: He lives at 2-6-4-9 Sunset Street.

Example: He lives at 26-49 Sunset Street.

Example: She hopes 19-92 will be a better year than 19-91.

Example: The 49ers won 14-to-6.

Example: Doctor Barbara Mueller is the featured speaker.

Turn to the next page for Abbreviations Test #1.

Abbreviations Test #1

Look over each column and decide which one contains the correct broadcast news treatment of abbreviations.

Column A	Column B	Column C
SOS	S-O-S	Save Our Ship
NCAA	N-C-double-A	Nat. Col. Ath. Assn.
294-4340	2-9-4-43-40	2944340
St.	Street	Strt.
Dr. Tim Wolf	Doctor Tim Wolf	Dct. Tim Wolf
Mister Jim Smith	Mr. Jim Smith	Mst. Jim Smith
1941	19-41	Nineteen-Forty-One
9865 North Ave.	9-8-6-5 North Avenue	9865 N. Ave.
Miz Grace Limbag	Ms. Grace Limbag	Mz. Grace Limbag
WHO-TV	W-H-O-T-V	Who-TV
Calif.	California	CA
Fri.	Friday	Fry-day
Eur.	Europe	Eupe
Lt. Jim Holtzman	Lieutenant Jim Holtzman	Ltnt. Jim Holtzman

If you think column A is the correct one, turn to page 49.

If you think column B is the correct one, turn to page 50.

If you think column C is the correct one, turn to page 51.

Column A? Not quite. Not one of the entries in column A is really acceptable broadcast news style. Remember to spell out words completely and to place hyphens between letters and numbers that you want the newscaster to pronounce individually.

Go back and look at column B again. It's the correct way to handle abbreviations in broadcast news. After you do that, turn to Abbreviations Test #2 on page 50.

Way to go! Column B is the correct broadcast news style. Putting hyphens between numbers and letters that you want individually pronounced and spelling out the names of days, months, states, countries, addresses, and most titles is the best way to ensure that what you want to say gets said.

Abbreviations Test #2

Now rewrite the following sentences in correct broadcast news style.

A. Jane Anderson has resigned from CBS and is now working for KOMU-TV, the NBC affiliate in Columbia, Mo.

B. Atty. Edward Whittler, 2347 E. West Ave., is a member of the NAACP.

C. LSU was defeated by BYU, 114-98.

D. Rev. J. J. Jefferson Jr. left the U.S. to live in the U.S.S.R. in 1973.

E. If you have any information, call 232-6677.

F. Lt. J. Thomas Forster says Sgt. John Riker is a hero.

G. Dr. Tim Kelly, 5491 Streeter Blvd., is the new Pres. of the Midcity YMCA.

Check your answers on page 52.

Column C is the worst of the three.

Go back and reread the section on abbreviations. Remember to spell out all words and to place hyphens between numbers and letters you want the newscaster to pronounce individually.

After you have reread the section, take another look at column B. It's the correct broadcast news style. After you do that, do Abbreviations Test #2 on page 50.

Answers to Abbreviations Test #2

A. **Rewrite:** Jane Anderson has resigned from C-B-S and is now working for K-O-M-U-T-V . . . the N-B-C affiliate in Columbia, Missouri.

B. **Rewrite:** Attorney Edward Whittler of 23-47 East West Avenue is a member of the N-double-A-C-P.

C. **Rewrite:** B-Y-U defeated L-S-U 114-to-98.

(Did you remember to reverse the teams to avoid a passive verb? You could spell out *Brigham Young University* and *Louisiana State University,* too!)

D. **Rewrite:** In 19-73, Reverend J-J Jefferson Junior left the United States to live in the Soviet Union.

(*Russia* would be okay instead of *Soviet Union.*)

E. **Rewrite:** Lieutenant J. Thomas Forster says Sergeant Riker is a hero.

(Did you spell *lieutenant* and *sergeant* correctly?)

F. **Rewrite:** Doctor Tim Kelly, of 54-91 Streeter Boulevard, is the new president of the Midcity Y-M-C-A.

(Did you spell out *Doctor*? *5-4-9-1* would be okay instead of *54-91*. Did you spell *Boulevard* correctly?)

How'd you do? If you missed more than two, you'd better go back and reread the appropriate sections. After you've done that, or if you missed two or less, turn to the next page.

• NUMBERS

By the Numbers

Numbers provide some additional problems for the broadcast newswriter. Numbers are hard to read aloud—especially long, involved numbers—so try to write numbers in a way that will help the newscaster read them easily. Here are some guidelines to follow.

For the single-digit numbers *one* through *nine*, write them out as words.

Examples: one, two, three . . . seven, eight, nine.

For the double-digit and triple-digit numbers *10* through *999*, use arabic numerals.

Examples: 10, 11 . . . 27 . . . 100 . . . 563 . . . 812 . . . 946 . . . 999

For all the rest of the numbers, use word-numeral combinations. Be sure to write out the words *million, billion, trillion*. Write out *hundred* only if the number is greater than one-thousand. A newscaster shouldn't have to think about numbers. Make them easy to read.

Be sure to include a hyphen between numbers and the words *thousand, million, billion, trillion*. Linking the parts of a number with hyphens keeps it together and helps ensure that a newscaster will read it correctly.

Examples: one-thousand,   one-thousand-and-one,   one-thousand-10,   11-hundred,   15-hundred,

two-thousand, 26-hundred-25, 10-thousand, 100-thousand, 147-thousand-673, 999-thousand, one-million,

one-million-217-thousand,   17-million-seven-thousand,   900-million,   one-billion,   10-and-a-half-billion,

438-billion-six-million, 654-billion-339-million-146-thousand-272

Ban the Symbols

Don't use any *symbols* in broadcast newswriting. SPELL OUT words like *dollars* and *cents*. Writing out a word instead of using a symbol makes it easier for the newscaster to read it.

Example: 123-dollars, **not** $123

Example: 10-cents, **not** 10¢ or .10

Example: number, **not** # or No.

Example: percent, **not** %

Example: and, **not** &

When you're dealing with measurements or amounts, be sure to SPELL OUT words like *inches, feet, yards, miles, acres, meters, ounces, pounds, tons, pints, quarts, gallons, degrees.*

Examples: three-inches, 10-feet, 47-yards, 26-miles, 616-acres, 36-meters, 12-ounces, 255-pounds, 16-tons, two-pints, one-quart, 50-gallons, 72-degrees

Ordinary Ordinals

Use *st, nd, rd, th* after numbers used in dates, addresses, and wherever else an ordinal is needed. We use our same number rules, of course. Single digits are written out as words. Double-digit and triple-digit numbers are written using numerals and the appropriate letter sounds.

Examples: first, June Second, June Third, Fifth Avenue, eighth, June 12th, June 21st, 29th place, 41st, 52nd time, 65th Street, 83rd, 110th, 221st, 333rd, 442nd

Bits and Pieces

Use our basic number rules for fractions and percentages. Remember to SPELL OUT the *point* too.

Example: 12-point-five-million

Example: 12-and-a-half-million

Example: one-third

Example: 33-percent

Example: three-fourths or three-quarters

Example: 75-percent

Example: one-16th

Round Figures

Don't be afraid to round off numbers to make them easier to understand. If it's 1,604, it's perfectly okay to write "about 16-hundred." You can round off numbers in most instances, but sometimes you'll want to be specific. Don't round off numbers when you report deaths or whenever specific figures are more meaningful.

When using rounded-off numbers, you should use words like *more than, nearly, about,* and *slightly less than* to let your listeners know you're not using EXACT figures.

Example: 593 **becomes** nearly 600

Example: 3,489 **becomes** about 35-hundred

Example: 13,323 **becomes** about 13-thousand-300

Example: 687,982 **becomes** almost 700-thousand

Example: 1,000,550 **becomes** more than one-million

Example: 999,879 **becomes** slightly less than one-million

Telling Time

We've already seen how time can often be an important element in a story. Write time so the newscaster can read it easily. When you use *o'clock* in your copy, write out the number preceding it. Do this even with 10, 11, and 12.

Examples: one o'clock . . . two o'clock . . . five o'clock . . . nine o'clock . . . ten o'clock . . . eleven o'clock . . . twelve o'clock

When you're dealing with hours, minutes, and seconds, use our basic number rules.

Example: Magee ran the mile in four-minutes-and-13-seconds.

Example: The kissing marathon lasted 72-hours-and-nine-minutes.

Example: Her time was two-hours-10-minutes-and-eight-seconds.

When you report time, NEVER use *A.M.* or *P.M.* Instead use *this morning, tomorrow evening, tonight, tomorrow afternoon,* and similar terms. They're more conversational. In addition, use numerals for hours and minutes notation.

Example: 5:30 this morning, **not** 5:30 A.M.

Example: 6:15 yesterday evening, **not** 6:15 P.M. yesterday

Example: 8:00 tonight, **not** 8:00 P.M.

Exceptions to Numbers Rules

As you've probably noticed, there are some exceptions to our rules for numbers. Times of day (hours and minutes), addresses, and phone numbers can be written using numerals even if they are less than nine.

Example: 7:30

Example: 1-1-1-6 Daffodil Road

Example: 2-3-2-23-97

Example: 2-3-2-2-3-9-7

In addition, don't start a sentence with a numeral. If you want to begin a sentence with a number, SPELL OUT the number even if it's greater than nine. Don't use numerals at the beginning of a sentence. It looks odd and could be confusing.

Example (poor): 25 people died in the accident.

Example (better): Twenty-five people died in the accident.

One last thing to remember. You SPELL OUT *hundred* only when the number is greater than one-thousand. When the number is less than one-thousand, use numerals.

Example: 1,300 **becomes** one-thousand-300 *or* 13-hundred

Example: 600 **DOES NOT become** 6-hundred *or* six-hundred

Numbers Test #1

Look over the following three groups of numbers. Pick out the one that has *all* the numbers written in correct broadcast news style.

Group A: one, six, 15, six-hundred, 897, 1,500, 1/4, $16, 8-billion

Group B: one, six, 15, 600, 897, 15-hundred, one-fourth, 16-dollars, eight-billion

Group C: one, 6, fifteen, 600, eight-hundred-97, 1,500, one-fourth, sixteen-dollars, 8,000,000,000

If you think group A is correct, turn to page 57.

If you think group B is correct, turn to page 58.

If you think group C is correct, turn to page 59.

Group A? Maybe it wasn't clear that 10 through 999 are written out as arabic numerals.

Six-hundred should be *600*.

1,500 should be *15-hundred*.

1/4 should be *one-fourth*.

$16 should be *16-dollars*.

8-billion should be *eight-billion*.

You'd better go back and reread the section on numbers. It's important to know how to write them correctly. Numbers are hard to read aloud, so you have to write them in a way that makes them somewhat easier.

After you reread the section, turn to page 58.

You said group B, and you're right. All of the numbers are written in broadcast news style. Try the next group of numbers.

Numbers Test #2

Look over the following list of numbers. If a number is written correctly, place an X in the blank. If a number is written incorrectly, correct it.

A. seven _____

B. ten _____

C. 17 _____

D. twenty-eight _____

E. 83 _____

F. one-hundred _____

G. 3-hundred-76 _____

H. 1,246 _____

I. 25-hundred _____

J. six-hundred-thousand _____

K. 3-million _____

L. $14,000 _____

M. 25-cents _____

N. 1/2 _____

O. one-fourth _____

P. June 24 _____

Q. 1st prize _____

R. 1022 22 Avenue _____

S. 50% _____

T. 11:15 P.M. tomorrow night _____

Check your answers on page 60.

Group C?

6 should be *six.*

Fifteen should be *15.*

Eight-hundred-97 should be *897.*

1,500 should be *15-hundred.*

Sixteen-dollars should be *16-dollars.*

8,000,000,000 should be *eight-billion.*

You'd better go back and reread the section on numbers. It's important to know how to write numbers correctly. They're hard enough to read aloud, so you should try to make them as easy to read as possible.

After rereading the section on numbers, turn to page 58.

Answers to Numbers Test #2

A. seven: *X*

B. ten: *10*

C. 17: *X*

D. twenty-eight: *28*

E. 83: *X*

F. one-hundred: *100*

G. 3-hundred-76: *376*

H. 1,246: *one-thousand-246* or *12-hundred-46*

I. 25-hundred: *X* or *two-thousand-500*

J. six-hundred-thousand: *600-thousand*

K. 3-million: *three-million*

L. $14,000: *14-thousand-dollars*

M. 25-cents: *X*

N. 1/2: *one-half* or *50-percent*

O. one-fourth: *X* or *25-percent* or *one-quarter*

P. June 24: *June 24th*

Q. 1st prize: *first prize*

R. 1022 22 Avenue: *10-22 22nd Avenue*

S. 50%: *50-percent* or *one-half*

T. 11:15 P.M. tomorrow night: *11:15 tomorrow night*

If you missed more than two, go back and reread the entire section on numbers and take the test again. If you missed two or less, you're ready for bigger things.

Go on to the next page.

Approximation Test

You're heading into the home stretch on numbers. All you have to do is round off or approximate the following numbers using proper broadcast news style.

A. 1,616 _____

B. 9.48 million _____

C. 9,487 _____

D. 49.96% _____

E. 297 yds. _____

F. 1,989 lbs. _____

G. 15.96 oz. (liquid) _____

H. 5,751,837 _____

I. 101% increase _____

J. 24¢ _____

K. 5,278 ft. _____

L. 97 _____

M. $75,193 _____

N. 11.82 in. _____

O. 8.2368 _____

Answers to Approximation Test

I used *about* for all the approximations, but any of the appropriate approximation words—*nearly, slightly more than,* or *slightly less than*—would be acceptable. The important thing is to be sure to let your listeners know you are approximating.

A. 1,616 **becomes** about 16-hundred *or* about one-thousand-600

B. 9.48 million **becomes** about nine-point-five-million *or* about nine-and-a-half-million *or* about nine-million-500-thousand

C. 9,487 **becomes** about 95-hundred *or* about nine-thousand-500

D. 49.96% **becomes** about 50-percent *or* about one-half

E. 297 yds. **becomes** about 300-yards

F. 1,989 lbs. **becomes** about two-thousand-pounds *or* about a ton

G. 15.96 oz. (liquid) **becomes** about 16-ounces *or* about a pint

H. 5,751,837 **becomes** about five-million-750-thousand *or* about five-point-75-million *or* about five-and-three-quarter-million

I. 101% increase **becomes** about a 100-percent increase *or* about double *or* about twice as much

J. 24¢ **becomes** about 25-cents *or* about a quarter

K. 5,278 ft. **becomes** about 53-hundred-feet *or* about a mile *or* about five-thousand-300-feet

L. 97 **becomes** about 100

M. $75,193 **becomes** about 75-thousand-dollars

N. 11.82 in. **becomes** about 12-inches *or* about a foot

O. 8.2368 **becomes** about eight-point-two-five *or* about eight-and-a-quarter

• PUNCTUATION

Practical Punctuation

Punctuation has one purpose in broadcast newswriting—to help the newscaster read the copy more easily and better. Most punctuation in broadcast newswriting is limited to the period, dash, question mark, and comma.

Three periods (. . .) are good to use when you want to indicate a pause. A dash (--) can do the same thing. A dash is often used instead of parentheses in broadcast newswriting.

Example: According to researchers at Midcity University . . . broccoli could be the next wonder food.

Scientists from the National Institute for Clinical Education--better known as NICE--say a daily dose of

broccoli might help us all live longer . . . but more tests are needed.

Don't be afraid to "dot" and "dash" up your copy. The more readable it is, the better it is.

• COPYEDITING

Correctable Errors

Some wise man once said, "To err is human." If that's true, broadcast newswriters are among the most human humans in the world. I'm talking about typographical errors now, not factual or content errors.

No matter how good a typist you are, when you get in a hurry or start thinking faster than you type, you're bound to start making mistakes. Computers have made it a lot easier to make corrections, of course, but you might not always have the time to reprint a flawed script. In such cases, you'll have to make corrections on the copy that's already been printed.

You may already know the copyediting symbols that are used in newspaper writing. Well, FORGET THEM. Forget them in broadcast newswriting, anyway.

Seeing something like the following isn't going to help the newscaster much. In fact, it will probably just confuse him.

"He smeled." *or* "He smelled like old an bull."

This won't help either: sheild.

Example: Do it this way . . . OR do it this this way.

If your copy starts to look like a giant roller coaster, you're better off blacking out the entire sentence and writing it over.

Try to keep your copy as clean as possible. Clean copy is easier to read. The following are other examples of broadcast news style editing.

Example: He will fly to Washington tomorrow.

Example: The Dodgers beat the ~~Prites~~ Pirates 4-to-1.

of Maple Street
Example: Lester Warren died in the accident.

- **SCRIPT STYLE**

    Putting It on Paper

    Nearly every radio and television station has a scripting style that's a little different from any other, but for the rest of this learning experience, you'll be using the following format.

    1. Type or write on full-size sheets of paper—8 1/2 x 11.

    2. Type or write on one side of the paper only.

    3. Double-space copy.

    4. Use uppercase and lowercase letters.

    5. If you type, use a 60-space (or 60-character) line: 20 lines of 60 spaces each equals about one minute of copy; 200 words equals about one minute.

    6. Use separate sheets of paper for each story.

    7. Don't divide words or numbers or hyphenated phrases at the end of a line and continue them on the next line. End each line with a complete word.

    8. Slug each story in the upper left-hand corner with a one-word or two-word summary of what the story is about, followed by your name and the date.

    Example: Fire deaths
    Wulfemeyer
    3/10/93

- ## SUMMARY

  ### Play It Again

  Look over the following summary of what we've covered so far in this learning experience. After you've done that, you'll be ready to take a stab at writing some stories.

  1. Don't parrot source copy. Use your own words.
  2. Write short sentences, but keep a natural conversational flow.
  3. Trim excess words.
  4. Write tightly, but explain the significance of the story and include all the important details.
  5. Use simple words.
  6. Don't cram sentences full of separate facts. Take facts one at a time, a sentence at a time.
  7. Make your copy easy on the ear *and* easy on the eye.
  8. Leads should set the tone of each story. Write them so they could logically follow, "Hey, Jill, guess what I just heard."
  9. Make sure you have all names spelled correctly.
  10. Include pronunciation guides for difficult names and words.
  11. Place titles before names. Extremely long titles can be broken up or placed after a name.
  12. Place ages before names. Use ages only when they're important to the story or when you don't have any other way to identify a person.
  13. Place addresses after names and say "who lives at" or "of."
  14. Attribution always comes before what was said.
  15. Don't worry about synonyms for *says* or *said*.
  16. Paraphrase direct quotes unless they're colorful.
  17. Don't be afraid to repeat words. There's no need to seek synonyms.
  18. Use personal pronouns.
  19. Use contractions.
  20. Use present tense, active voice verbs as often as possible.
  21. Beware of abbreviations. SPELL OUT words the way you want them to be read.
  22. Place time elements in sentences so they sound natural.
  23. Write numbers so they're easy to read.
  24. Round off numbers to make them more memorable.
  25. Take care with fractions and decimals. Make sure they're understandable.
  26. Don't use symbols. SPELL OUT $, ¢, %, &, #, and all the rest as words.
  27. Use punctuation to help the newscaster read your copy.
  28. Keep your copy clean.
  29. Don't use newspaper or copyediting symbols. Black out mistakes completely and print or retype corrections.
  30. Think and write the way you talk.

The BIG Time

If you don't feel you're ready to tackle writing a few stories on your own now, you might want to go back and glance over the sections where you think you're weak before taking the big plunge. If you feel confident and are ready to go, you can start by looking over the following suggestions for putting broadcast news stories together.

Remember what you've already learned about leads. They set the tone of your story. They should tell the listener what the story is going to be about.

After the lead, the rest is pretty much up to you. Depending on the type of information you're dealing with, you might want to follow up the lead with some of the specific details of the story. You should try to include all the important details and facts, or at least as many as you have time for.

Include the causes and reasons for actions, events, and statements. The WHY of every story is important. Someplace in your story be sure to include WHY the story is important. WHY it is significant. WHY it is newsworthy. And WHAT it means to the listeners.

Sometimes the WHY comes out of a story naturally. Other times you have to dig it out and point it out to your listeners. For example, if your city council just approved $900,000 for a new park, you'd want to explain what all the money is going for—specific things—and how much it's going to cost each individual taxpayer, as well as WHY the park is needed.

A good way to end a story is with some background information. You might mention some of the things that led up to the event you're reporting. If you're talking about a person, you might mention some of his or her other jobs, titles, or accomplishments. You might mention some of the lesser details or possible future developments that might be caused by the event, action, or statement you're writing about. You also might mention what the next step will be or likely will be.

Don't forget to include the source of your information—the attribution—if the subject matter requires it.

Keep these suggestions in mind as you look over the information on page 67. For the next few writing assignments, pretend you are a newswriter for a radio station in Midcity. Midcity could be in any state.

●　**EXERCISES**

Komodo Dragons Story

Write a 20-second story on the Komodo dragons' new home. If you're typing, use a 60-space line. Seven FULL lines should be about 20 seconds. If you're writing out the story in longhand, about 75 words should equal 20 seconds.

MIDCITY ZOO

FOR IMMEDIATE RELEASE
CONTACT: CAROLE TOWNE

PUBLIC AFFAIRS

A moat filled with "dragons" was unveiled for the public at the Midcity Zoo today--but the moat was not the kind associated with medieval castles, and the dragons were not mythological monsters but real live reptiles.

The moat is part of an exhibit just completed that will house the Zoo's two Komodo dragons, the world's largest lizards from the Indonesian island of Komodo and surrounding smaller islands. The reptiles were released into their new home today by Lt. General Victor Krulak, president of the Midcity Zoological Society, and Jerry H. Staedeli, Zoo reptile curator.

The new exhibit, adjacent to the Zoo's present Reptile House, was built at a cost of $154,000 and measures sixty by thirty feet. It features enclosed, radiant-heated quarters for the dragons, a pool, extensive landscaping, and a 6-foot-deep moat across which Zoo visitors view the lizards.

The $154,000 was donated to the Zoological Society by the Dorothy Chang Foundation of Midcity.

The dragons had been in their heated indoor quarters for a day to allow them time to become acclimated to that part of their new exhibit. Today was the first time the reptiles were allowed access to the exhibit's outdoor areas.

##########

After you've written your story, turn to the next page to see how one broadcast newswriter handled it.

Komodo Dragons Story Model

Zoo dragons
wulf
4/20/93

(Koh-MOH-doh)

The Komodo dragons at the Midcity Zoo have a new

home. It's right next to the Reptile House and it has

all the comforts--radiant heat . . . a pool . . . lots of plants

and a six-foot-deep moat to keep out unwanted visitors.

All that luxury cost the zoo 154-thousand-dollars. The

Dorothy Chang Foundation donated the money. Komodo

dragons come from Indonesia and are the world's largest

lizards.

#########

Let's analyze this story. You compare your version as we go through the various elements of the story.

1. The lead sets the tone for the story. It tells what the story is about.
2. After the lead, we get some details: where the exhibit is, what it has, how much it cost, and where the money came from.
3. The story ends with a little background information—what Komodo dragons are and where they come from. This is a good way to get out of a story. It's a natural ending. What more is there to say that's really important?

Endings are sometimes difficult to write. It's hard to decide what information to end with. *Sound* has a lot to do with it. After you've written a few stories, you'll get to where you'll be able to *hear* the ending.

You'll put a sentence together and it will just *sound* like the logical place to end the story. When you're reading over the source copy, keep alert for such information. It sometimes makes writing easier if you know what you're going to end with before you start writing.

Did you remember to include a pronunciation guide for Komodo? Did you bother to look it up? Remember, it helps the newscaster if you include how to pronounce unknown or unusual names or words.

Did you use the proper style for writing numbers? (*two* dragons, *six*-foot-deep moat, *60-by-30*-feet, *154-thousand*-dollars)

If you used Victor Krulak, did you put his title in the right place and SPELL OUT *Lieutenant*? Remember, titles come before names.

Did you change the sentence about where the money came from into an active voice sentence?

If you follow all the guidelines in this workbook, your stories will be easy for the newscaster to read and easy for the listeners to understand.

Record your story and the model. Play them back and decide which one *sounds* better to you.

Try writing another 20-second story from the information on the next page. You obtained the information after talking with your sources at the Midcity Police Department.

Traffic Fatality Story

(All information obtained from Midcity Police Department.)

Traffic accident at 7:43 A.M. today.

Only one car involved.

Two men killed.

Names have not been released pending notification of next of kin.

Accident occurred near Northside Recreation Center.

Driver apparently lost control of car after trying to avoid something on Carson Ave.

45-ft. of skid marks were found at scene leading to the spot where car left road.

Car, a late model Ford, left roadway, traveled up a slight embankment, hit a telephone pole, and flipped over.

"The driver obviously just lost control of the car and couldn't keep it on the road," according to Sgt. Jane Sanders, Midcity Police spokesperson.

The fatalities were number 45 and 46 in Midcity so far this year.

##########

After you've written your story, turn to the model on the next page.

Traffic Fatality Story Model

Traffic deaths
Kelly
5/3/93

Two men died in a one-car accident this morning near

the Northside Recreation Center. Police say the driver

probably tried to avoid something on the road and lost

control of the car. It skidded 45-feet . . . ran up a slight

hill . . . hit a telephone pole . . . and flipped over. The

names of the men won't be released until their families

have been notified. Midcity's traffic death toll is now

46 for the year.

##########

Let's analyze this story.

1.   Right at the start we find out what happened: two men died in a traffic accident. This story could start with a verbless lead, too.

Example: Two more traffic deaths in Midcity this morning.

Both the verbless and the emphasis lead could logically follow, "Hey Jack, did you hear?"

2.   After the lead, we get some details—how the accident probably happened and the fact that the names haven't been released yet. Did you modify the formal and stilted, "pending notification of next of kin"? People don't talk this way, so don't write this way. Write conversationally.

3.   The story ends with a form of background information—the number of people who have died in traffic accidents so far this year. Does it seem like a logical place to end?

Did you use the quote from the police spokesperson? It really doesn't add much does it? You probably do need some attribution for the information about the cause of the accident. The exact cause hasn't been proven yet.
Record your story and the model. How do they *sound*?

Try another 20-second story. It's on the next page.

Cancer Money Story

(Research)

(Washington)--A PROFESSOR AT THE UNIVERSITY OF IOWA'S SCHOOL OF MEDICINE SAID TODAY THERE SHOULD BE A 150-MILLION DOLLAR INCREASE FOR CANCER RESEARCH FOR NEXT YEAR. APPEARING BEFORE THE SENATE APPROPRIATIONS COMMITTEE IN WASHINGTON, D.C., DR. AARON SHIPPEN TESTIFIED THE MONEY WOULD BE USED FOR FINDING AN EFFECTIVE CURE FOR CANCER. CURRENTLY, THE ADMINISTRATION HAS BUDGETED 500-MILLION DOLLARS FOR NEXT YEAR. SHIPPEN IS ARGUING THAT SUBSEQUENT CONSULTATIONS WITH OTHER CANCER ORGANIZATIONS AND PROGRAM DIRECTORS CONVINCED HIM THAT THE CURRENT BUDGET IS TOO LOW, THAT ANOTHER 150-MILLION DOLLARS CAN AND SHOULD BE EFFECTIVELY USED. SHIPPEN ADDED THAT THE 150-MILLION DOLLAR INCREASE SHOULD BE ALLOCATED FOR GRANTS IN THE FIELD OF CANCER RESEARCH.

###########

After you've finished writing your story, turn to the next page and look at the way a professional newswriter handled it.

Cancer Money Story Model

Cancer money
McFadden
6-10-93

A University of Iowa professor says the Federal

Government should kick in another 150-million-dollars for

cancer research next year. Doctor Aaron Shippen of

Iowa's School of Medicine told a U-S Senate Committee

that the 500-million-dollars already budgeted is not

enough. He says the extra money is needed to pay for

research grants so an effective cancer cure can be found.

##########

Let's analyze this story.

1.   The lead tells what the story is about—more federal money needed for cancer research. (At least Dr. Shippen thinks so.) We find out WHO says more money is needed, HOW MUCH money is needed, and WHEN it's needed.

2.   In the second sentence we get some details—WHY the money is needed and TO WHOM Dr. Shippen directed his plea.

3.   In the last sentence we find out WHAT the extra money would be used for and another part of WHY it's needed—to find an effective cure for cancer.

How does your story compare? Do you have as much information? Is it clear and easy to understand? Did you use the proper style for all of the numbers? Did you use delayed identification and start the story with Dr. Shippen's title rather than his name?

Record your story and the model. Is yours as easy on the ear?

Look over the source copy on the next page. Write a 30-second story from it. That's 10 lines of typed copy, or 100 words.

Sports Arena Story

(BLOOMBERG)

(Midcity)--THE MIDCITY BOARD OF SUPERVISORS LAST NIGHT DIRECTED CITY CLERK ABBEY OSTREM TO PERFORM VALIDATION CHECKS OF SIGNATURES ON PETITIONS IN THAT DRIVE AGAINST DR. LAWRENCE BLOOMBERG'S SPORTS WORLD DEVELOPMENT. PRIOR TO LAST NIGHT, "CITIZENS CONCERNED FOR MIDCITY," A LOCAL ACTIVIST GROUP, HAD TURNED IN 3,000 SIGNATURES IN AN ATTEMPT TO PUT THE DEVELOPMENT TO A PUBLIC VOTE. LAST MONTH, SUPERVISORS GAVE TENTATIVE APPROVAL FOR THE DEVELOPMENT THAT INCLUDES SINGLE-FAMILY HOMES, CONDOMINIUMS, AND A SHOPPING PLAZA. THE DEVELOPMENT WOULD CENTER ON A SPORTS ARENA FOR BLOOMBERG'S PROFESSIONAL BASKETBALL TEAM, THE MIDCITY MAVERICKS, OF THE WORLD BASKETBALL ASSOCIATION. LAST NIGHT CITIZENS CONCERNED FOR MIDCITY TURNED IN ANOTHER 1,900 SIGNATURES, ACCORDING TO BOARD SPOKESPERSON ROBERT SCOTT. ONLY 3,500 SIGNATURES ARE NEEDED TO BRING THE ISSUE TO A VOTE. IF THE CITY CLERK VALIDATES THE APPROPRIATE NUMBER OF SIGNATURES, THE PUBLIC VOTE WILL BE HELD 3 WEEKS FROM TOMORROW, SAID SCOTT.

##########

After you've written your story, look over the model on the next page.

Sports Arena Story Model

Bloomberg
wulfemeyer
11/28/84

The Board of Supervisors wants the city clerk to check
the signatures on petitions in that drive to stop Doctor
Lawrence Bloomberg's Sports World development. A group
called Citizens Concerned for Midcity has been collecting
names to force a public vote on the issue. The group has
already collected about five-thousand signatures . . . and only
35-hundred are needed.

Bloomberg wants to build a sports arena for his Midcity
Mavericks of the World Basketball Association at the center
of the housing and shopping development.

If enough of the signatures are valid, the vote will be
held three weeks from tomorrow.

##########

Let's analyze this story.

1. Once again the lead tells what the story is going to be about. We get the names of all the
participants and the parts they're playing in this little drama.
2. We find out how many signatures have been turned in and how many are needed to bring the issue
to a vote.
3. We also get a little background information to finish off the story, just in case some of the listeners
haven't been keeping up with what undoubtedly has been a very prominent and ongoing story. In addition,
we get some information about what is likely to happen next and when the vote might be taken.

The source copy is a little confusing, and there is at least one major element missing: WHY. Why does
the citizens group want to block the project? You'll come across these gaping holes in source copy often.
If you can, fill them by making phone calls or checking other sources. If you can't fill them, do the best you
can with what you have.

How did your story come out? Did you have trouble getting through the source copy? It is difficult. If
you got the number of signatures collected and the number needed (using the proper style), if you
mentioned the citizens group in connection with the drive to stop the development, and if you included poor
old Dr. Bloomberg, you did a good job.

Did you add up the two figures that dealt with the number of signatures? About 3,000 were turned in
originally and another 1,900 were added, which brings the grand total to about 5,000. You owe it to your
listeners to do this simple addition. Be on the lookout for ways to simplify numbers. Check their accuracy,
too! Make sure they make sense and make sure they're correct.

Record the source copy, your story, and the model. How do they *sound*? The source copy was
supposedly written for broadcast. Do you think it's very listenable? How about your story? The model?

Try another 30-second story over the source copy on the next page.

Supervisor Controversy Story

City of Midcity
MEMORANDUM

File No.: 2796
To: News Media
From: Carl Johnson, Assistant to the Mayor
Subject: Mayor Jack Shelley's response to "Weak Supervisor" claim

You have requested Mayor Shelley's response to Supervisor Donna Loren's testimony to the Charter Revision Committee Tuesday night as reported in the Midcity Times.

The following is the Mayor's statement:

"I think it is nonsense to suggest, as Ms. Donna Loren has done, that those members of the Board of Supervisors who were appointed are weaker than those who were elected. Since their appointment, each of the four supervisors Ms. Loren refers to has run or has vowed to run for election.

"So each has had the courage to come before the voters.

"Now neither Ms. Loren nor I have participated in the appointment of a Board member. But I greatly doubt that appointees are selected on the basis of being 'least offensive' as Ms. Loren suggests. That certainly would not be the criterion I would apply, and I'm certain this Board would look to qualifications and appoint the person it felt most qualified. Some of the Board's strongest members have been appointed.

"Finally, I would agree with Ms. Loren that if a Board is weak, it is not because of form or structure. The only real limitation on legislative power is the legislator's initiative, imagination, and persuasiveness."

cc: members of the Board of Supervisors

##########

After you've written your story, check the model on the next page.

Supervisor Controversy Story Model

shelley/loren
mac
7-29-93

Mayor Shelley says Supervisor Donna Loren's claim that
the four appointed members of the Board of Supervisors are
weaker than the elected members is a bunch of nonsense. In
fact . . . Shelley says some of the Board's strongest members
have been appointed. He says the four were picked not
because they were the least offensive as Loren
suggests . . . but because they were the most qualified people
available. And Shelley says since their appointment . . . each
of the four has run or has promised to run for election.
Loren made her accusations at the Charter Revision Committee
hearing Tuesday night.

##########

Let's analyze this story.

1. The lead gives the listeners the whole story in a nutshell. The mayor thinks Supervisor Loren is full of baloney.
2. Next comes the mayor's justification for his statements. (Appointed members are some of the strongest. They were the most qualified. They have run or are running for election.)
3. The writer ties the story off with a little background information. (What started the whole thing—Loren's claims at the Charter Revision hearing.)

In this kind of story, you can probably assume that most of your listeners know something about Loren's charges, so you can start your story with the mayor's response.

It would be perfectly correct if you started the story with something like "Mayor Shelley has responded to Supervisor Loren's claim that the four appointed members of the Board of Supervisors are weaker than the elected members. Shelley says the charge is a bunch of nonsense."

Remember, there are several "correct" ways to write this story or any other story for that matter. The important thing is to get the vital, significant information out to the listeners. The model stories and all the other material in this learning experience are designed to help you do just that, and to do it in a way that is easy for the newscaster to read and easy for the listener to understand.

Record your story and the model story. How do they *sound*? Does yours sound as good? Better?

The best way to improve your writing is to write, write, write, and write some more. After you have the basics down, you just have to keep writing until it starts to come easy for you.

You might have had some problems writing the stories in this workbook. It might have taken you more time than you would have liked. Don't feel too bad. After you've written 40 to 50 stories, you'll start to get the hang of it.

Try writing one more 30-second story from the copy on the next page. You're still working in Midcity.

USO Story

(CHAPIN/USO)

(Midcity)--THE MIDCITY USO SAYS IT WANTS THE $100,000.00 OR MORE ALLEGEDLY PROMISED TO IT BY GARY CHAPIN, THE ORGANIZER OF THE "COAST GUARD GIFT PAC" PROGRAM. AN ATTORNEY FOR THE USO SAID HE'S WRITTEN TO THE STATE ATTORNEY GENERAL TO FORCE CHAPIN TO HAND OVER THE MONEY. HE SAID CHAPIN PROMISED TO GIVE THE USO A PERCENTAGE OF THE PROCEEDS FROM THE "GIFT PAC" PROJECT, IN WHICH CHAPIN SOLICITED DONATIONS HE USED TO SEND PRESENTS TO COAST GUARDSMEN. CHAPIN NOW SAYS HE CAN'T PAY SINCE A LATER PROGRAM OF HIS CALLED "HELP FOR NAVY WIDOWS" IS $100,000.00 IN DEBT. IN THE "NAVY WIDOWS" PROGRAM, CHAPIN PROPOSED TO GIVE EACH WIDOW A CAR AND A FREE VACATION. NO DECISION FROM THE STATE ATTORNEY GENERAL IS EXPECTED FOR AT LEAST 30 DAYS.

##########

After you've written your story, turn to the next page for a look at the model story.

USO Story Model

        Chapin/USO
        wulfemeyer
        12-5-93

                        (CHAY-pihn)

        The Midcity U-S-O says Gary Chapin owes it at least

100-thousand-dollars. Chapin organized the "Coast Guard Gift

Pac" program . . . and the U-S-O says he promised it some money

from the proceeds. Chapin says he doesn't have the money,

because one of his other projects . . . "Help for Navy

Widows" . . . is in the red. An attorney for the U-S-O is asking

the State Attorney General to help clear up the problem. No

decision is expected for at least a month, though. In the

"Gift Pac" program . . . Chapin sent presents to Coast Guardsmen.

In the "Navy Widows" program . . . he wanted to give each widow a

new car and a free vacation.

                        #########

Let's analyze this story.

1.   The lead tells what the story is going to be about.

2.   The facts of the story come next—the promises, the programs and their failures, and what the USO plans to do to get its money.

3.   At the end, a little background information is provided to help the listeners remember who Chapin is.

I hope you remembered the correct form for writing numbers and you remembered to put hyphens between U-S-O. You're writing for the ear—so your listeners will understand your story easily—but you're also trying to write so the newscaster will be able to read your copy easily.
        Record all three of the versions—source, your own, and the model. Do they all *sound* the same, or is one better than the others? Why do you think one is better? What is it about the one that *sounds* good to you that is different from the others?

Enter the wonderful world of writing for television in the next section.

P A R T 3

Adding Visuals

- ## WRITING FOR TELEVISION

Turn on the TV

By making it this far, you're well on your way to mastering the basic techniques of broadcast newswriting. With a bit more practice, you should be able to write simple "reader" stories for both radio and television newscasts. A "reader" story is one that is read by the newscaster without any additional audio or video enhancement—no sound bites from sources, no pictures, no maps, no charts, and no video.

Before we finish this self-instructional learning experience, I want to give you an opportunity to try your hand at writing some slightly more complex stories. Writing copy to go with pictures, graphics, and video involves all of the concerns we've addressed so far, plus you have to be careful to match the words with whatever viewers are seeing on the TV screen.

There are three basic ways that copy can be written for pictures and other visuals.

1. The story is written first, then the visuals are selected, edited, and placed to match the words.
2. The visuals are selected and edited first, then the words are written to match the visuals.
3. The words and visuals are considered simultaneously with appropriate compromises being made to achieve the most effective and frequent matching of words and visuals.

If you can master writing to match pre-selected and pre-edited visuals, you'll easily be able to master the other two methods. The key to matching words and visuals is to look at the visuals or a description of the visuals and determine what information is most closely associated with what visuals.

You don't want to be overly descriptive about what viewers are seeing, but you do want to explain what they're seeing and avoid blatant conflicts between what they're seeing and what they're hearing.

Example (poor):	Picture of Martin Boyd	Linda Smith will take over next month.
Example (better):	Picture of Martin Boyd	Martin Boyd will step down next month.

When writing to match video, look at the order of the separate scenes to get a sense of how the story will have to flow. Make written or mental notes about what places, actions, and people come before what other places, actions, and people. Begin formulating your story so that you can be sure to match the major participants in the video as well as major shifts in subject matter or geographic location.

Example:	SHOT LIST
1. Fire trucks and flames	:06
2. Fire Captain (Garver)	:03
3. Burning house	:03
4. Homeowner (McFeely)	:06
5. Dog (Sparky)	:06
TOTAL TIME:	:24

Using the example shot list, you'd first have to write some general information about the fire. Then, in order, you'd have to mention the Fire Captain, the house, the homeowner, and the significance of the dog.

Once you have the order figured out, you have to concern yourself with matching the words with the visuals. Using the example, you'd need six seconds of information about the fire, the location, and the firefighting effort. Next, you'd need three seconds of information about the Fire Captain, three seconds about the house, six seconds about the homeowner, and six seconds about Sparky, the dog. Remember, a FULL line of 60 spaces equals three seconds.

Example:

TAKE VIDEO/VO   The fire started at about six o'clock and it took

firefighters almost two hours to bring it under

control.

Fire Captain Brenda Garver estimated about

125-thousand-dollars damage was done to the house.

John McFeely says his dog Sparky's barking woke

him up in time to get his family out of the burning

house.

McFeely says Sparky's reward is going to be a new

dog house and steak dinners for a week.

Don't forget that pauses can be used to help you improve your matching of words and pictures. A picture really can be worth a thousand words, especially if the picture has natural sound with it.

Keep pauses to a minimum, though. They should not be overused and are best when video is dramatic and natural sound helps viewers understand what's going on.

Pauses can be inserted in your script in the following ways:

Example: . . . . (Pause :03) . . . .

Example: . . . .

Example: . . . . (Pause until plane takes off) . . . .

Be sure to place parentheses around words you don't want the newscaster to read.

As you write your story, be sure to check the timing. If you fall behind the visuals, eliminate some words or even whole sentences. If you get ahead of the visuals, add some words or put in some pauses.

Split Screen

The script format for television writing is somewhat different from radio writing. In most television stations, copy is written down the middle of the page so that newscasters will be able to read it easily when it's projected onto the lens of the camera via a teleprompter system. Viewers don't see the words, of course, but newscasters do and it helps them maintain eye contact with viewers.

In this learning experience, we'll use a modified style for our television scripts. Using one-second or two-second lines takes quite a bit of paper. In an effort to save a few trees, we'll still use 60-space lines, but we'll shift the copy that we want the newscaster to read to the right **two-thirds** of the paper. Down the left **one-third** of the paper, we'll include directions to the technicians who help us get the newscast on the air. Write the directions in ALL CAPS!

Example:

TALENT:	An earthquake rocked Egypt this morning. No deaths or injuries reported, but lots of damage--at least 150-million-dollars worth.

TAKE MAP/VO FULL SCREEN	The center of the quake was about a mile north of Cairo, but people felt the earth move 100 miles away.

TALENT:	The earthquake measured five-point-nine on the Richter Scale.

Example:

TALENT:	An earthquake rocked Egypt this morning.

TAKE VIDEO/VO	No deaths or injuries reported, but lots of damage--at least 150-million-dollars worth. The center of the quake was about a mile north of Cairo, but people felt the earth move 100 miles away.

TALENT:	The earthquake measured five-point-nine on the Richter Scale.

In the example scripts, TALENT is used to indicate when you want the newscaster to be seen on-camera reading copy. When you want a director to show a picture, map, or chart or to roll video, draw a heavy line and then tell her to TAKE MAP, TAKE PICTURE, TAKE CHART, or TAKE VIDEO. The VO stands for voice-over and means that the newscaster continues to read even though viewers don't see her. FULL SCREEN is included when you want the picture, map, or chart to fill the entire television screen rather than be used as an insert over the newscaster's shoulder. Be sure to draw heavy lines between changes in what viewers are supposed to see. Every time you move from TALENT to something else and vice versa, draw a heavy line. It'll help avoid embarrassing moments for newscasters, directors, and you.

• EXERCISES

Westlake High School Story

Now it's time to write some copy to match a pre-selected map. Take a look at the source copy and the description of the map. Write a 15-second story. That's about five FULL lines of copy or about 50 words. Remember, we're still using 60-space lines. Each FULL line equals three seconds. Be sure to indicate where the map should be inserted. Follow the script format used for the earthquake story on the previous page.

FULL SCREEN MAP:

Highway 95 runs north and south. Madison Avenue runs east and west. Site for high school colored in red.

SOURCE COPY:

(1) Site for the construction of the new Westlake High School has been selected by the Midcity Board of Education.
(2) 75-acre parcel.
(3) Location is near the intersection of Highway 95 and Madison Ave.
(4) Site selected because of proximity to Highway 95 and service via bus line.
(5) Cost: $25,000,000.
(6) Cost covers land, construction, furniture, and other facilities and equipment.

After you've written your story, look at the model story on the next page.

Westlake High School Story Model

Westlake HS
Rodriquez
6/3/93

TALENT   The Midcity Board of Education has decided where

the new Westlake High School will be built.

TAKE MAP   The Board picked a 75-acre Madison Avenue location,

FULL SCREEN   because it's near Highway 95 and it's on the bus line.

TALENT: The new Westlake High School will cost about

25-million-dollars.

##########

Let's analyze this story.

1. The lead gets right to the news: The Board of Education has picked the site for the new high school.

2. The second sentence deals with the precise location of the site. Since that's what the map shows, it is inserted so viewers can hear and see just where the school will be built.

3. After a mention of why the site was selected, we return to the newscaster for information about how much the new school will cost taxpayers.

Did you remember the proper style for *25-million-dollars* and *75-acre* site? Did you spell out *Avenue?* Record your version and the model. Which one sounds better? Why?

Try writing another story that uses a full-screen graphic. Turn to the next page.

SAT Scores Story

Write a 30-second story from the following information. Be sure to insert the chart when you write about the specific test scores.

Full Screen Chart:

SAT Scores

	Last Year	This Year
Midcity	940	960
Nation	950	950

Information:

(1) Last year's nationwide average on Scholastic Aptitude Test (SAT) = 950.

(2) Last year's Midcity average on SAT = 940.

(3) This year's nationwide average on SAT = 950.

(4) This year's Midcity average on SAT = 960.

(5) First time in a decade that average Midcity SAT scores are higher than national average.

(6) Total possible on SAT = 1,600.

(7) 2nd straight year Midcity SAT scores have increased.

(8) Quote from Midcity School District spokesperson Courtney Lynn:

"Our teachers made a commitment three years ago to help students improve their SAT scores and it looks as if the effort is really paying off. We feel the scores will continue to increase more next year and for many years to come."

(9) Test is taken by high school seniors.

(10) One program given credit for the improved SAT scores is the required fifteen minutes of "free reading" time every day at local high schools, according to Lynn. The program has been in operation for four years.

After you've written your story, check out the model story on the next page.

SAT Scores Story Model

Test Scores
Buckalew
6/10/93

TALENT:	More proof that Midcity schools are doing something right. For the second straight year, the Scholastic Aptitude Test scores of local high school seniors are up.

TAKE SCORES FULL SCREEN	The average this year was 960 out of a possible 16-hundred. Last year the average was 940. The increase pushed the local scores above the national average for the first time in 10 years.

TALENT:	School district officials say Midcity teachers have worked hard to help students improve their test scores. Officials expect the scores to increase even more next year.

##########

An analysis of this story is on the next page.

Let's analyze this story.

1.   The lead is a conclusion. Based on the increasing test scores, the writer concludes that local schools must be doing something right.

2.   The second sentence is more like a traditional lead. The phrase at the beginning of the sentence could be moved to the end, but at least we get some information about SAT scores, who takes the test, and the upward trend.

3.   After stating the general direction of the scores, the writer gets more specific. The chart is inserted as the newscaster talks about the exact numbers and the move past the national average.

4.   Finally, after the chart is taken out, the writer explains why the scores have increased and includes the prediction that scores will be even better next year.

Did you write all the numbers in correct broadcast news style? (*second, 960, 950, 940, 16-hundred, 10*) Did you use the information about the "free reading" period? It might be worth including.

How does your version compare to the model? Record them both and play them back. Which is more conversational? Remember that we still want the copy to flow in a natural, conversational manner even though we have pictures to worry about.

Let's complicate things even more. Try writing a 30-second "voice-over" story from the information on the next page. A voice-over is a story that is read by a newscaster while video is seen by the viewers. Remember to look at the shot list to get an idea of the order of the scenes. Organize the information to match the video as closely as possible.

Include some on-camera newscaster copy before and after the 18 seconds of video. The newscaster copy that comes before the video is called an *intro* (short for introduction) and the newscaster copy that comes after the video is called a *tag* or *tail*. You should have about six lines of video copy and about four lines of on-camera newscaster copy.

Measles Shots Story

SHOT LIST:

(1) Long shot of people standing in line at the health center	:06
(2) Medium shot of two mothers holding their children	:03
(3) Medium shot of college student getting a shot	:06
(4) Close up shot of college student's reaction to shot	:03

                                        TOTAL   :18

Information:

(1) At 8:00 A.M. this morning, Eastside Medical Center began giving free measles immunizations. Session ended at 12:00 P.M.

(2) Free measles shots will be given again next Monday, starting at 8:00 A.M.

(3) Midcity University requires that freshmen students provide proof of measles immunization before they are permitted to register for classes.

(4) Most of the shots given to persons younger than 12 years old, but about 33% went to college-age students.

(5) 5,023 immunizations given.

(6) Quote from Dr. Eric Wulfemeyer, director of the Eastside Medical Center:

"We've pretty much got measles under control, but we still have to be sure everyone has been immunized. We feel it's important that we do our part to help keep Midcity a healthy place to live and work."

(7) Eastside Medical Center used its own money to provide the shots.

(8) There were five reported cases of measles in Midcity last year, according to Midcity Department of Public Health.

As usual, the model story is on the next page.

Measles Shots Story Model

Kim
Free Shots
7/9/93

TALENT:	Lots of Midcitians got a shot in the arm this morning.

TAKE VIDEO/VO	More than five-thousand people got free measles immunizations at the Eastside Medical Center.
	Most of the shots went to kids, of course, but some college students showed up, too. Midcity University requires that incoming freshmen be immunized against measles before they can sign up for classes.

TALENT:	If you missed out on the measles shots today, the Eastside Medical Center will be giving free measles immunizations again next Monday morning starting at eight o'clock.

#########

An analysis of this story is on the next page.

Let's analyze this story.

1.   The writer takes a few liberties with the lead, but it's interesting and will likely grab interest. The lead is a bit vague, but perhaps the viewers will want to find out just what "shot in the arm" means.

2.   The first video scene of people in line runs six seconds, so the writer decided to include information about the location and the number of people who received shots. She needed two lines to fill the time and came pretty close.

3.   The next scene of two mothers and their children runs just three seconds. The writer decided to mention the point that most of the people who received shots were children. Good matching!

4.   The third scene of a college student receiving a shot runs six seconds. Here the writer mentions the twist on a fairly routine story. Even though most people think of children when the subject of measles shots comes up, college students need to be immunized, too. Again, good matching!

5.   The fourth scene is just three seconds long. Since it is a continuation of the college student getting a shot, the writer continues with information related to why students need shots.

6.   After the video ends, the writer has the newscaster give information about the next round of free shots. Sounds like a good ending, don't you think?

Overall, the matching of audio and video is pretty good. How did you do? Did yours match as well? You needed two lines of copy (or copy plus pauses) for the first scene, one line for the second scene, two lines for the third scene, and one line for the fourth scene.

Did you look at the shot list to get an idea of how you had to order the information? Did you recognize that you had to start with some general information about the location and number of people who received shots and then mention kids before giving the information about college students?

Record your version and the model. How do they sound? Matching video while still maintaining a logical, conversational flow in your copy is a real art. Don't feel too bad if you had trouble with this story. With more practice, you'll improve.

Try another voice-over story. The shot list and information are on the next page. The entire story should run 45 seconds (15 seconds of on-camera newscaster copy and 30 seconds of copy to go with the video). Be sure to include some on-camera newscaster copy before and after the video. You should have about 10 lines of video copy and about five lines of on-camera newscaster copy.

Delayed Debate Story

SHOT LIST:

(1) Wide shot of almost empty auditorium	:06
(2) Close-up of clock (7:55)	:03
(3) Medium shot of one bored person/empty seats	:03
(4) Medium shot of Sanchez and Dozier	:03
(5) Wide shot of sparse audience	:03
(6) Close-up of Sanchez	:06
(7) Close-up of Dozier	:06
TOTAL	:30

Information:

(1) Scheduled debate between Board of Supervisors candidates Maria Sanchez and David Dozier did not start on time tonight.

(2) Candidates will debate again tomorrow night at 7:00 P.M. at the Southside Recreation Center. Both vowed to be on time for that one.

(3) Both candidates had attended dinner meetings and were late getting to McFadden Elementary School. Spokespersons for candidates said scheduling conflicts were the real culprits. The candidates simply are trying to attend too many functions and when one event runs long, it affects all the others.

(4) Debate was supposed to start at 7:00 P.M., but candidates did not show up until 7:55!

(5) Pretty good crowd on hand at 7:00—about 150—but by the time the candidates arrived, only about 15 people were still there.

(6) Candidates are running in District Four.

(7) After some discussion, Sanchez and Dozier decided to go ahead with the debate.

(8) Usual issues debated.

(9) One new issue did come up, though. Sanchez said we had to do something to stimulate construction in Midcity. She suggested eliminating the fees charged in connection with building permits. Dozier didn't like that idea. He said such a move would cost the city way too much money. He said he'd consider cutting the fees in half, but that would be as far as he'd go.

After you've written your story, go to the next page for a look at the model story.

Delayed Debate Story Model

Candidate Problems
Washington
10/10/93

TALENT:	Some scheduling problems hit two supervisor candidates this evening and they ended up playing to an almost empty house at McFadden Elementary School.

TAKE VIDEO/VO	A debate between the two District Four candidates was supposed to start at seven o'clock, but neither one showed up until almost 8:00. By that time, most of the people who had wanted to hear the candidates had left.
	Both Maria Sanchez and David Dozier were delayed at dinner meetings. When the debate finally started, Sanchez said she favors waiving building permit fees so we'll get more construction going here.
	Dozier countered that completely waiving fees was too drastic. He suggested cutting the fees in half.

TALENT:	The next Sanchez-Dozier debate is scheduled for tomorrow night at 7:00 at the Southside Recreation Center and the candidates promise to be on time.

#########

An analysis of this story is on the next page.

Let's analyze the candidate debate story.

1. The lead tells what happened. A couple of supervisor candidates had some problems and were late to a scheduled debate. Their tardiness cost them most of their audience.

2. The first scene of video is of the empty auditorium and runs :06. The writer mentions what was supposed to happen and when.

3. The second scene of the clock runs :03 and is matched well with copy about the hour delay.

4. The third scene of a bored, diehard political groupie and a bunch of empty seats runs :03, so the writer mentions the absent throngs.

5. The fourth scene of the tardy candidates runs :03, so logically the candidates should be mentioned here. They are.

6. The fifth scene is what's known as a "cutaway." It's a general scene that is used as a transition between two main scenes. Usually you don't have to match cutaways, so the writer simply continues with details of why the candidates were late.

7. The sixth scene of Maria Sanchez runs :06. Whenever a major participant appears in video, he or she should be mentioned. She is.

8. The seventh scene of David Dozier runs :06. The writer does a good job of matching Dozier with information about what he said.

9. Once we come back to the on-camera newscaster, the writer concludes with information about the next debate. Seems like a logical ending doesn't it?

How does your version compare with the model? Did you match as often and as well? Did you have the information in the right order? You had to write about the empty room first (:06), then the time problem (:03), the sparse crowd (:03), the arrival of the candidates (:03 + :03), comments from Sanchez (:06), and comments from Dozier (:06).

Did you write all the times in correct style (7:00, 8:00, seven o'clock)? Did your story flow in a conversational manner?

Record your version and the model. How do they sound? Do they sound as if you're *telling* a story rather than *reading* a story?

Try a rewrite of your story if you don't feel you matched well and/or the conversational flow was not all that it could have been.

Don't forget all the things we've worked on during this learning experience to help the poor old newscaster make some sense of your prose. You might even be the person who has to read your copy, and you have to write well so you can broadcast well.

If you or another newscaster has trouble reading your copy, you can be sure your listeners are going to have even more trouble understanding it. Make your copy easy on the eye as well as easy on the ear.

I know you could go on writing broadcast news stories for hours, but that's enough for now. But before you put the workbook away, take one last look at a summary of the material we've covered in this broadcast newswriting learning experience.

- ## SUMMARY

Once Again, Dear Friends

1. Write it your way—in your own words. Don't parrot source copy.

2. Write the way you talk.

3. Be brief, but include all the important information.

4. Use simple, easy-to-understand words.

5. Don't stuff your sentences full of separate facts.

6. Your lead should set the tone for the story. It's like a headline.

7. Write the way you talk.

8. Include pronunciation guides for unusual names and words.

9. Place titles before names.

10. Place attribution before what was said.

11. Place ages before names.

12. Write the way you talk.

13. Use contractions and personal pronouns.

14. Use present tense verbs whenever you can.

15. Use active voice verbs instead of passive voice verbs.

16. Don't abbreviate. Write out all words as you want them read.

17. Write the way you talk.

18. Write numbers so they're easy to read and understand.

19. Put hyphens between numbers/letters you want pronounced separately.

20. Use punctuation to help the newscaster read your copy easily.

21. Keep your copy clean.

22. Write the way you talk.

23. Limit your use of copyediting symbols.

24. Match words with pictures, graphics and video.

25. Write the way you talk.

• CONGRATULATIONS

Give yourself a pat on the back for successfully completing this self-instructional learning experience. You've worked hard and done well.

Keep practicing, though. Schedule time to write at least one story every day. Take newspaper stories and try to write them in broadcast news style.

Listen to radio newscasts and television newscasts as often as you can. Analyze and think critically about the way stories are written. Take notes on the stories and try to write your own versions.

Attend events that you know will receive broadcast news coverage. Take notes and write stories based on the events. Compare your stories to the ones that air on local stations.

Work for campus radio and television stations. See if you can intern or volunteer at local stations. Public broadcasting stations almost always are looking for bright, energetic people to volunteer their time.

There's really no substitute for practicing the craft of broadcast newswriting. Just do it!

• ADDITIONAL READING

Listed below are some books that will help you become a better broadcast newswriter.

Air Words: Writing for Broadcast News by John Hewitt
The Broadcast News Process by Frederick Shook and Dan Lattimore
Broadcast Newswriting by David Keith Cohler
Broadcast Newswriting: A Workbook by K. Tim Wulfemeyer
Broadcast News Writing and Reporting by Peter E. Mayeux
Broadcast Newswriting as Process by J. Clark Weaver
Newswriting for the Electronic Media by Daniel E. Garvey and William L. Rivers
Rewriting Network News by Mervin Block
Writing Broadcast News—Shorter, Sharper, Stronger by Mervin Block
Writing News for Broadcast by Edward Bliss, Jr., and John M. Patterson

• APPENDIX

United Press International Pronunciation Guide

VOWELS

A   AY for long A as in *mate*
     A for short A as in *cat*
     AI for nasal A as in *air*
     AH for short A as in *father*
     AW for broad A as in *talk*

E   EE for long E as in *meet*
     EH for short E as in *get*
     UH for hollow E as in *the*
     AY for French long E with
       accent as in *Pathé*
     IH for E as in *pretty*
     EW for EW as in *few*
     E for middle E as in *per*

O   OH for long O as in *note* or *though*
     AW for broad O as in *fought*
     AH for short O as in *hot*
     OO for O as in *fool* or *through*
     U for O as in *foot*
     OW for O as in *how* or *plough*

U   EW for long U as in *mule*
     OO for long U as in *rule*
       U for middle U as in *put*
     UH for short U as in *shut*

I   EYE for long I as in *time*
     EE for French long I as in *machine*
     IH for short I as in *pity*

CONSONANTS

K for hard C as in *cat*
S for soft C as in *cease*
SH for soft CH as in *machine*
CH for hard CH or TCH as in *catch*
Z for hard S as in *disease*
S for soft S as in *sun*
G for hard G as in *gang*
J for soft G as in *general*